CAPTAIN
MARK PHILLIPS
ON RIDING

1 The author riding Out and About at Crookham in 1983

CAPTAIN MARK PHILLIPS ON RIDING

Captain Mark Phillips

with Jane Kidd

An Arco Equestrian Book
Prentice Hall Press New York

Published in 1987 by Prentice Hall Press
A Division of Simon & Schuster, Inc.
Gulf & Western Building
One Gulf & Western Plaza
New York, NY 10023

Originally published by Stanley Paul & Company Limited,
an imprint of Century Hutchinson Limited

PRENTICE HALL PRESS is a trademark of Simon & Schuster, Inc.

Library of Congress Cataloging in Publication Data
Phillips, Mark, 1948–
Captain Mark Phillips on riding,
Includes index.
1. Horsemanship,   I. Title,
SP309, P54 1986   798.2   86-91471
ISBN 0-13-114521-5

Printed and bound in Great Britain
10 9 8 7 7 5 4 3 2 1

First Prentice Hall Press Edition

CONTENTS

ACKNOWLEDGEMENTS

I should like to thank Jane Kidd for all her help in the preparation of the manuscript.

The author and publishers would like to thank Kit Houghton for all his excellent photographs and Patricia Frost for her line drawings.

PART 1
THE RIDING

1·HOW TO BEGIN

Riding has done so much for me. Through it I have made many friends, both nationally and internationally. I have travelled to countries all over the world. It has been character forming too; so many times when I think I am riding at my best I am again deposited on my backside. One week I may have won a major championship, the next fallen off at a local event. If nothing else riding horses is a great leveller which teaches you to appreciate the good and bad things in life.

Even for those who are not aiming for competitions there are the satisfactions of that personal relationship between a human and an animal. There is so much to be gained from riding, and I hope I can help you towards appreciating some of this by explaining a little about how I ride and train my horses.

THE TEACHER

Riding is like driving a motor-car – you have to know how to handle the steering, the accelerator and the brake. As with driving, someone is needed to explain the basics. Without the help of a teacher it would be dangerous for a beginner to get on a horse: the horse is stronger than a rider and capable of taking off at speed, so the rider must know how to exercise control.

It helps, too, if your teacher has sound basic knowledge, as early lessons have a tremendous influence on the way a person rides. I feel sorry for children with a bad seat as the usual reason for this is that they did not have a good teacher from the beginning. When I was on the leading rein there were constant cries from my mother of 'hands down', 'heels down', 'sit up', 'look up'. That was what gave me a reasonable seat and a good base from which to work in later years. It is so easy to learn bad habits and develop, for example, a cowboy seat with the legs forward. It is then so much more difficult to adapt later to the basic position which gives the best control over the horse.

There are many people who may be good riding teachers – parents, friends or professional instructors. The choice depends on the opportunities available and how the beginner feels after trying out a few lessons. If his or her confidence is growing and the lessons are enjoyable, then the choice is good. If the rider is frightened and not enjoying the lessons, then another instructor or maybe another horse must be found.

THE SCHOOL

When selecting a place to ride, talk to others who are learning, visit local riding schools and watch the lessons. Follow other people's advice, and judge by your own experience.

Approved riding schools are professional establishments and are usually the best places at which to learn, except for those fortunate enough to have a knowledgeable friend or parent or who find a yard in which to go and help. At home we have one or two young local people who join us during holidays. They like to be with horses and it is a good way for them to learn and to find out whether they would like to get more involved.

It is not just the knowledge of the teachers that helps beginners, it is also the environment. An indoor or enclosed outdoor school is ideal because the horses cannot go too fast. It is dangerous to start in a big field where horses easily get out of

3 Too big a pony for this small rider

4 Too small a pony for this rider

5 A good sized pony for the rider

control. Beginners should become competent enough to steer, stop and start in a confined area before venturing outside. Chapter 7 covers these first lessons.

THE HORSE

The horse or pony is another key to learning and with a good schoolmaster – a well trained, steady, experienced animal – there is less need for instruction. The first horse or pony has to be 'bomb-proof' so that the initial experience is not frightening, as a rider who has been frightened finds it difficult to relax, and tension inhibits learning. If beginners start off in the wrong way, then all too often things go from bad to worse and they very quickly give up riding. A sensible horse is needed so that the beginner can relax, enjoy the experience and, the chances are, continue riding for many years.

A horse with a 'bomb-proof' temperament is the most vital aid to learning, but it is pretty boring and tiring for a rider if he has to keep kicking to make his mount move. The ideal horse is one that is not so quiet that he will not go, nor one who is so energetic he will not stop. A balance must be struck.

Size is another factor, as it is important that the beginner feels comfortable. If the horse is too big, most beginners will be more nervous; if he is too small, it is more difficult for the rider to use the aids and keep his balance, and the poor horse has to work very hard.

Some people want to start off by owning their horse or pony, but it is far better to try out the horse scene first, either at a friend's stables or at a riding school, to find out what is involved in looking after a horse. Make sure you really enjoy it and then, if you are still determined to buy, take along a knowledgeable friend when you go to look at possible horses or ponies. There are some unscrupulous dealers who will sell you an unsuitable animal just to achieve a sale.

FACILITIES

Writing the cheque for the horse or pony is only the beginning. It is important to have a well-fenced field with some sort of shelter from the wind – a thick hedge will do – and look out, too, for dangerous weeds (see diagram overleaf) or objects on which a horse or pony could cut himself. There

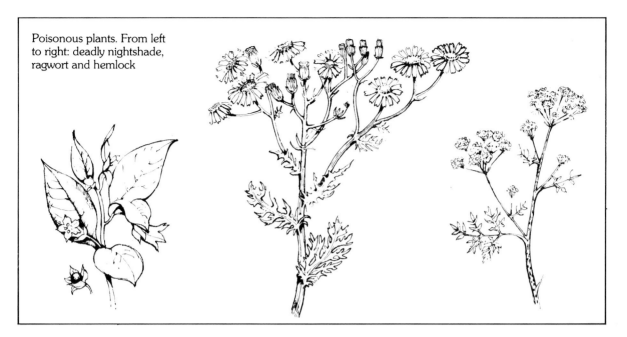

Poisonous plants. From left to right: deadly nightshade, ragwort and hemlock

6 As well as getting enjoyment from riding a pony, he can also be a great friend

must be a supply of fresh water, and when the grass runs out you will need a stock of hay and, if necessary, hard food. The horse or pony has to be wormed regularly, and a blacksmith will be needed to look after his feet and a vet to check his teeth. There are the financial outlays for all this, as well as for tack, insurance and personal clothing. All these requirements are discussed in more detail in the second section of this book.

This may sound pretty offputting, but your own horse is a friend who is always there, ready to be ridden whenever you want to enjoy yourself. Riding your own pony or horse means you can start to build up a relationship with him. He will be a companion who most of the time tries to please; but remember, he will always be there, even when you do not want him. Your own horse or pony can be great fun but he will also require constant attention.

Ponies are easier to look after than horses. They are less delicate, more able to fend for themselves and cheaper to feed. Children who are given their own ponies to look after usually become much more interested in riding, but parents still need to provide plenty of encouragement. It is unfair to expect small children to catch ponies who do not want to be caught, or who then tow them from one end of a field to the other. Even after they have captured them, small children cannot be expected to saddle up on their own if they are not strong enough to tighten the girth, and cannot reach the pony's head to put on the bridle. This is no fun, and children must enjoy their riding if they are to continue past their first lessons. It is incumbent upon the parents to make it as easy as possible for their children to ride. My parents made it very easy for me and therefore I enjoyed riding as a child. They did not allow me to be bullied by an animal much stronger than I was. I used to be given the choice of riding or going for a walk with nanny, and I always chose the former!

My own children had little control over their ponies when they started. I had to be careful that nothing frightening happened, that they enjoyed it and wanted to go on. It must not become another school lesson. I try to explain everything clearly and help them to find out that riding the right way makes it simpler. The correct ways soon become habits because they find it easier to ride that way. I try to explain to whoever I am teaching how and why I want something done, then when they try it out and it works they are pleased. This I find very satisfying.

The explanations are necessary but there is no substitute for experience, spending hours in the saddle, getting used to the feel of the animal and to using the controls. The more riding he does, the more likely the rider is to become relaxed, confident and competent.

Inevitably beginners have a spill, but falls are part of learning. As a boy I totted up eighty-four falls before I lost count. It is important to be relaxed and not be frightened of falling off. The actual experience of falling off is often the only way to help you conquer this fear. Whenever it is inevitable that you are about to hit the ground, it is essential not to resist, but to let yourself go, relax and, if possible, roll into a ball so that you can go over and over. In this way you do not hurt yourself so much.

7 It is important for parents to help catch and tack up the pony for small children

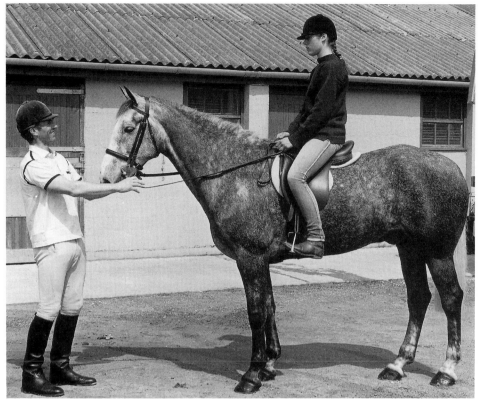

8 A rider sensibly equipped for first lessons

EQUIPMENT

The most vulnerable part of the body in a fall is the head. A good nationally approved hard hat is the only piece of equipment which beginners *must* have. It is important that it fits correctly, and official societies recommend, and some require, that a chin strap be worn.

Apart from a hat no other specialist equipment is essential in the early stages. A riding jacket will be needed if you start competing but until then any jacket is suitable as long as it does not make a noise, as some nylon ones do when anything is brushed against them. A sweater, shirt, blouse or sweat shirt can be worn when riding, in fact anything you feel relaxed or comfortable in and that does not inhibit the forward movement of the arms.

Gloves are advisable in the winter but are not necessary in the summer unless your hands are particularly soft and delicate.

Legs can easily be rubbed, so tight-fitting clothing is needed. If you are not using breeches or jodhpurs then it is advisable to wear a pair of tights under close-fitting jeans.

On the feet, rubber, bumpy-soled shoes are dangerous, because in falls often they stop the foot from slipping free of the stirrup. Leather-soled shoes are acceptable, but leather-soled boots are more comfortable.

I was not allowed to carry a whip until I was about thirteen and had to rely on my legs to make the pony go. Some ponies are very lazy and children do need a whip, but it must be used as an aid to forward momentum and not as a punishment.

Spurs are not a good idea for beginners as their legs are not under control and the spurs tend to be dug into the horse at random. It is only when the rider has achieved a good basic position, has control over the use of his legs, and knows how and when to apply the spurs that they should be worn.

The early stages of riding do not require an investment in specialized clothing, other than a hat. The important thing is to be comfortable (see photograph 8).

2 · THE HORSE

To become a competent rider it helps to know as much as possible about the horse – the terminology, the good and bad points and how he moves.

THE POINTS OF A HORSE

All horsemen look at the head to find out about a horse's character. Big ears and big eyes with a good width between them are signs of a genuine, kind temperament. A broad forehead is a sign of intelligence. On the other hand, small eyes are usually found on obstinate, ungenerous horses, and a bump between the eyes on wilful ones; small ears can often mean a difficult temperament which will need careful handling. The outline of the face is also important; a horse with a dishy face tends to

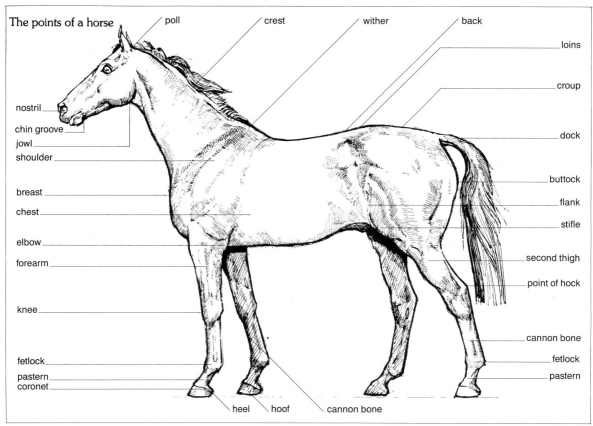

The points of a horse

poll   crest   wither   back

loins

croup

nostril

dock

chin groove
jowl
shoulder

buttock

breast

flank

chest

stifle

elbow

second thigh

forearm

point of hock

knee

cannon bone

fetlock

fetlock

pastern
coronet

pastern

heel   hoof   cannon bone

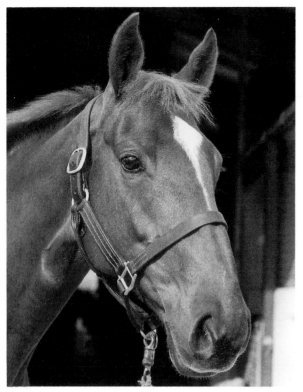

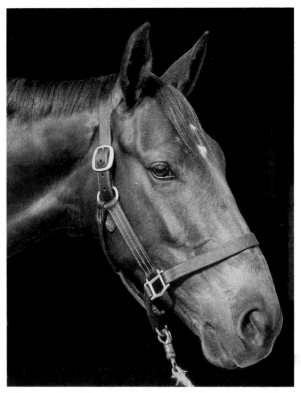

9 A good head with the indicators of a generous temperament, a bold eye and big ears

10 A nice head but not as good as the first photograph as the eye is not so generous and the ears are slightly smaller

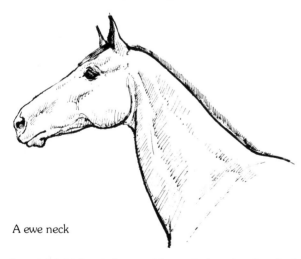

A ewe neck

be a bit 'chicken'; those with pretty heads often lack boldness. I like horses with a straight profile or even a larger, plainer head, as they tend to be genuine workmen.

If the horse has a ewe neck (see diagram) he tends to move like a giraffe and is difficult to control.

I like a neck to come out of the top of the shoulder in a smooth curve, as such a horse tends to be better balanced. If the neck is attached lower, so that the top of the shoulder is higher than the top of the neck, the horse tends to go on his forehand, does not move or jump so well and tends to 'lean on' or 'be heavy' in the rider's hand.

The withers should be clearly defined – if they are flat the saddle tends to slip forward over them. Also, horses with flat withers usually carry more weight on the forehand which puts a strain on the front legs, as well as tending to be not such a comfortable ride.

A good slope to the shoulder enables the forelegs to move more freely and fluently. If the shoulder is upright, the action tends to be more stiff and stilted.

The short-coupled horse tends to be stronger in the back, more powerful and athletic, like the compact gymnast, but at the same time it is often stiffer than the longer backed horse. The latter can bend more easily and tends to be the better

11 A well proportioned horse with good depth to his body. He has a Roman nose, the ears are big, but the *eye* is not particularly generous. His muscles are a little too developed under his neck to make it easy to get him on the bit. The shoulder is a little straight. He has a short coupled body with good quarters. The hocks could be closer to the ground. The front leg is well made but a shorter cannon bone would be preferable

galloper, but in the extreme the longer the back the weaker it becomes.

In the quarters a good width between the hip bones gives the horse more strength. The quarters are the source of power so it helps if they are muscular, broad and with a gently sloping croup (see photograph 11).

A horse should carry his tail well. If it is tucked in, it is a possible sign of a back injury or at least that his movement is shuffling.

In the hind legs, a strong second thigh and hocks which are close to the ground give the horse more power. Cow hocks are rarely much of a problem nor are a pair of curbs, but bowed or sickle hocks tend to be weak. I prefer straight hocks.

Horses who are deep through the body (measured from the wither to the belly) usually have more stamina, but too much breadth tends to make the body too heavy for the limbs. This is called 'heavy topped'. At the same time I am wary of a horse that is so narrow that the front legs move very close together, as then there is little room for the heart and lungs (the organs essential for stamina), and the forelegs often brush one another.

Well-proportioned joints, with no signs of puffiness or bony growths, are best as they are less likely to cause lameness. A horse whose front legs are concave, especially at the knees (known as back at the knee), is more prone to tendon strain than a horse with a more convex shape (over at the knee).

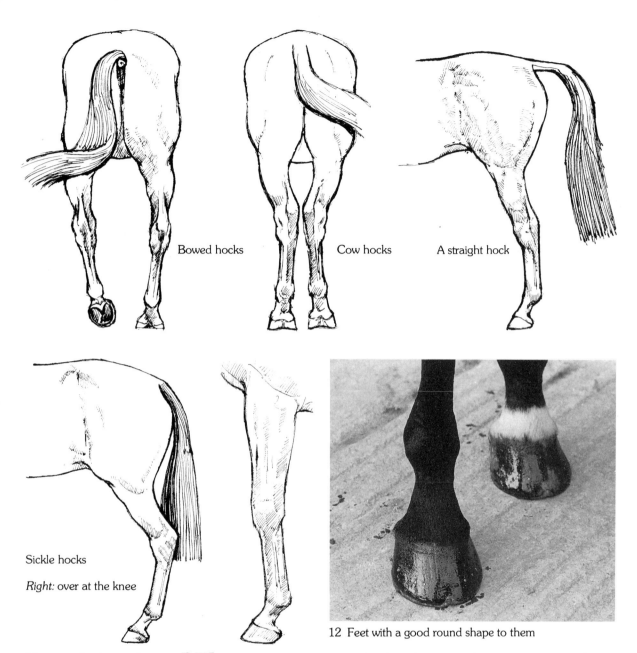

Bowed hocks

Cow hocks

A straight hock

Sickle hocks

Right: over at the knee

12 Feet with a good round shape to them

Horses who have short cannon bones are usually the soundest, especially if they are over at the knee, as the tendons then are shorter, thicker and therefore stronger.

Upright pasterns result in a less than perfect suspension system: the horse will be subjected to more jarring and is more liable to strain his joints. On the other hand, although the horse with long sloping pasterns is more comfortable to ride, unfor-tunately this shape results in more strain being placed on the tendons. Therefore a gently sloping pastern is the most desirable.

With feet I am wary of the two extremes. Boxy, narrow, upright feet are more inclined to develop bone disorders (navicular, side bones and ring bones) whilst wide flat feet are more liable to bruis-ing. The round foot is what I like (*see* photograph 12).

It is the proportions of the horse which are so important. All the components should be put together so that they are balanced and in harmony. A long neck on a short body will make it difficult for the horse to stay in balance, as will the reverse arrangement. The general impression should be that he is well proportioned. The better proportioned the horse, the more of an athlete he is likely to be.

The beginner is not going to subject his horse to the same strains as a competition rider so many of the above weaknesses are acceptable in a schoolmaster, as long as the weakness is compensated for by strong surrounding areas.

What is important is that the horse should have a good outlook as this is the key to temperament. Good temperament is probably the number one priority for beginners. The horse is not going to be asked to clear huge fences in the jumping arena or produce great extensions in a dressage test. He needs to be the type who will look after his rider, a willing character who when kicked goes forward, when pulled stops, and who does not shy at every piece of paper and tin can on the roadside.

THE PACES

Horses have three different paces: the walk, the trot and the canter, with the gallop being an extended variation of the canter. Some breeds have unusual gaits such as the running walk, the amble and the pace, but these are not common; most horses have simply the three basic gaits.

In all the paces the ideal is a horse who moves his limbs straight forward and back when viewed from the front or rear. A disher (who throws the feet outwards) is acceptable if the movement is not too pronounced, but pigeon-toed horses (feet turning inwards) tend to put more pressure and therefore strain on the outside of their joints. Horses who move close behind are stronger than those who are wide behind.

Daisy-cutters (those with extravagant but stiff movement of the forelegs) are flashy but find it difficult to handle deep going. I like best the horse with a rounded action, when all the joints in the limbs flex, but without too much knee action.

The walk should be free and easy, not a stiff shuffle. Four hoofbeats should be heard at equal intervals. When the left foreleg is lifted off the ground, the next to lift is the right hindleg, then the right foreleg followed by the left hindleg, all at equal intervals.

The trot is best when it is smooth and comfortable. Long-striding extravagant movers need an exceptionally supple rider to stay with the movement, while those with short, stiff strides and tense backs bounce their riders up and down.

When trotting, the horse moves his legs in diagonal pairs (left fore and right hind together, right fore and left hind together), so that just two hoofbeats are heard. One diagonal pair of feet leave the ground just before the other touches it, so there is a moment of suspension, and it is this lifting period which beginners find difficult to sit to in the saddle. By rising out of the saddle every other stride (in rising trot) this problem is avoided, once the rider has learnt to go up and down, up and down, up and down in time with the horse's movement.

13 The walk which is a marching gait in four time

14–15 The trot showing how the legs move in diagonal pairs. However the outline is not correct as the poll should be the highest point

16–17 *Right:* The canter showing the up down movement in each stride. This horse is rather strong in the hand and therefore not very well balanced resulting (see bottom photograph) in him going behind the bit

In a good canter the horse takes balanced, smooth strides which are even in length and neither too long nor too choppy. In this pace three hoof-beats are heard and each stride is separated from the next by a moment of suspension. In the canter the fore and hind legs on one side will reach further forward than the pair on the other side. A horse is said to be 'on the right leg' if the right legs are leading, or 'on the left leg' if the left legs are leading. In a circle or turn he is said to be 'on the correct leg' if the inside legs are leading.

When the horse is on the right leg, the left hind leg starts the sequence of a stride, lifting off the ground before the right hind and the left foreleg, which move together; last comes the right foreleg, followed by that moment of suspension. On the left leg, the right hind leg lifts, followed by the left hind and right foreleg, then the left foreleg, followed by a moment of suspension.

A canter is said to be disunited when this sequence is incorrect. For instance, a horse on the right lead may change in front to the left lead, but leave the hindlegs in the original sequence, so that the forehand is on one lead, the hindquarters on another. This feels uncomfortable and the horse will be unbalanced.

19 A good canter in which the horse is well balanced with the inside hind stepping well forward underneath the horse and the shoulder coming up off the ground

20 Lengthening the strides at the trot. Although the results are good the jockey is leaning back too much

18 *Left:* A good working trot. The hind leg is coming well forward underneath the horse who is balanced and carrying himself

The gallop is the fastest pace of the horse and is too fast for a beginner, especially if riding a horse who can really gallop. A learner driver might be able to manage a Mini at 50mph but would be very dangerous in a Jaguar at 100mph. In the gallop the canter strides become so extended that the diagonal sequence is broken, four hoofbeats being heard, followed by a moment of suspension. In gallop on the left leg, the right hind leg lifts first, then the left hind leg, the right foreleg, the left foreleg and finally the moment of suspension.

In each of the basic paces the horse can take longer or shorter strides and these all have names. When the strides are at their longest they are known as the extended walk, trot or canter; at their next longest, the medium walk, trot or canter; and at their shortest (and highest), the collected walk, trot or canter. A horse has to be very well trained to produce these differences without changing the rhythm. The tendency is to hurry when trying to lengthen and to slow down when trying to collect, but this results only in a change of speed not in the length of stride.

For beginners and young horses most riding is done at the working paces, which are those most natural for the horse. The strides are of a length which are longer than the collected and shorter than the medium. They are the working trot and canter. There is no working walk, as in the walk there is not so much scope to change the length of the strides; it would be difficult to distinguish a fourth type, so the basic work is done in medium walk.

TRANSITIONS

From this brief summary of the paces it will be realized that there is quite a range of variations in the types of pace. For instance, a horse can lengthen into medium trot, shorten into collected trot or change into a medium walk. All these changes of gear are known as transitions, whether they are within a pace or from one pace to another and will be discussed further in Chapter 9, Training the Horse and Pony.

3 · THE TACK

Having talked a little about the horse, the next step is to give some information about the basic equipment required.

The first thing to remember is that it pays to buy good-quality tack and to look after it. Leather that breaks can be dangerous and, at the very least, damaging. A broken rein put me out of Badminton one year. It went 'ping' as Persian Holiday pecked on landing over Huntman's Close. I only managed to stop when coming face to face with the tent for the ladies' loo! That was a hard way to find out about the importance of both buying good-quality tack and looking after it well.

THE HEADCOLLAR

The headcollar (known as the halter in America) is used for leading and tying up the horse (see diagram on page 93).

THE BRIDLE

The bridle which is used for riding can be a snaffle, curb, double or bitless; for beginners the snaffle is the most suitable.

The snaffle bridle consists of a headpiece and throatlash, two cheekpieces and a browband. The fit of the bridle can be adjusted by altering the buckles on one or both cheekpieces. The cheekpieces are attached to the rings of the bit, as are the reins.

NOSEBANDS

Separate from the bridle but attached through the brow band is the noseband which can be a cavesson (chin strap adjusted above the bit and below the protruding cheekbone); a drop (chin strap which is adjusted below the bit and which can be tightened to help prevent the mouth from opening and the jaw from crossing); a flash (cavesson chin strap plus thinner strap adjusted under the bit, which again can help to keep the mouth closed, see photograph 22); and the Grakle (chin straps which cross each

21 A snaffle bridle correctly fitted with a cavesson noseband

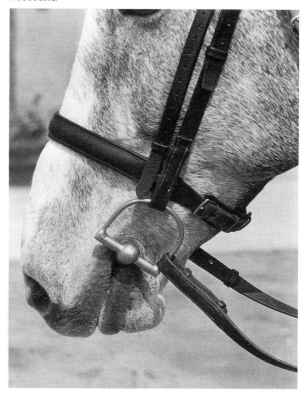

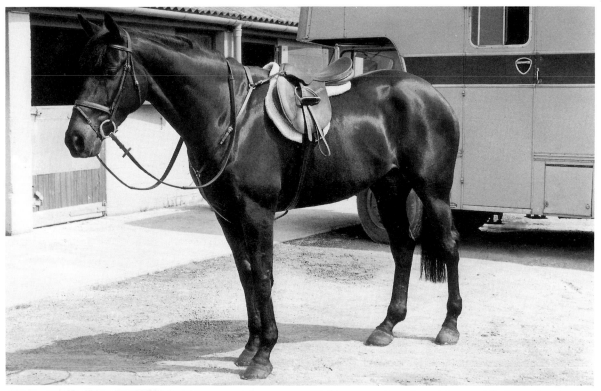

22 Horse wearing a breastplate and flash noseband

23 *Left:* Horse wearing no martingale, a snaffle bridle and Grakle noseband

other on the nasal bone where they must be pinned or stitched together, one to adjust under the bit and one above – the cross-over action provides the strongest means of keeping the mouth closed – see photograph 23).

THE BITS

The basic bit is the snaffle, of which there are numerous variations; depending on the design, they may be more or less severe, more or less likely to make a horse play with or take hold of the bit.

The mouthpiece is the most important section and the thinner it is the more severe it is. The material from which it is made also affects its severity, rubber being the mildest, followed by vulcanite and finally steel, which produces the strongest effect. In a snaffle the mouthpiece may be in one piece (mildest), have a single joint (stronger), or be double jointed (which makes it difficult for the horse to lean on the bit). The final consideration is the

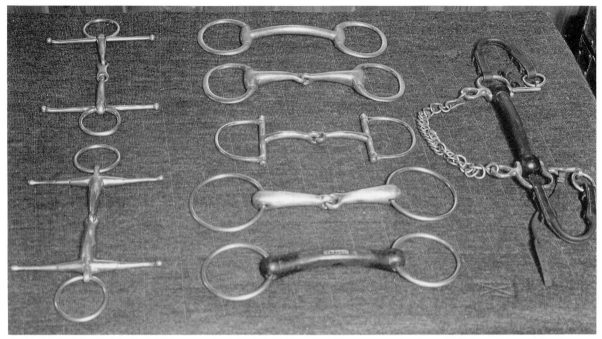

24 Some of the most common bits. *Bottom left:* a Fulmer snaffle. *Top left:* a double jointed snaffle with cheek pieces. *Centre from top to bottom:* a straight bar eggbut snaffle with metal mouthpiece, an eggbut snaffle, a 'D' ring racing snaffle with thin mouthpiece, a German snaffle, a loose ring snaffle with straight bar vulcanite mouthpiece. *Right:* a vulcanite Pelham with leather rounders so only one rein need be used

rings: if they are fixed at the side, as in an eggbut, they encourage the horse to catch hold of the bit; if they are loose (i.e. the rings run through holes in the ends of the mouthpiece so that there is movement), then horses tend to play more with the bit.

Curb bits are more severe than snaffles and often have to be used for hard-mouthed ponies, but they should not be necessary on well-trained horses (other than the double bridle in dressage and showing). Curb bits are stronger than snaffles because when the reins are pulled the curb chain tightens into the horse's chin groove and the bit has a lever effect, which puts pressure on both the mouth and on the poll of the curb bit. I prefer the Pelham, as it is mildest. The Kimblewick is very severe, and horses tend to lock their jaws in it.

Gags are used by some experienced riders but they are very severe and should not be used by beginners.

I very rarely use anything but snaffles and the simple formula for 'which bit?' is: if you cannot stop, try a thinner or multi-jointed metal mouthpiece. There is one proviso, however: I am sure horses

run towards pain so if the bit is *too* sharp, then they may pull even harder. If the horse will not take hold of the bit, try a thicker one; do not put a sharp bit on a horse who will not go.

The bit I use most is the loose-ring German snaffle. This is quite mild as the mouthpiece is thick, with a single joint, and the loose rings encourage the horse to champ and so 'mouth' the bit. If the horse is fussy or unsettled in his mouth and tends to rattle the mouthpiece then I try an eggbut. If a horse leans on the bit then a bit with some lift to its action is needed and a racing 'D' ring snaffle or a double-jointed snaffle may be appropriate. Horses who pull hard, with their heads in the air, often go much better in a straight bar vulcanite snaffle. This encourages the horse to accept the bit with a lower, more controllable head carriage.

Some horses respond to a curb bit. A Pelham is often a good bit for ponies but rounders (see photograph 24) should be used as it is difficult for a child or beginner to cope with four reins.

When following the principle that there is a bit to counter most problems, before changing a bit check that the problem does not lie in other areas.

If the rider is not balanced or is using his hands roughly, then the horse may be objecting to him, not to the bit. Many mouth problems are related to the rider's shortcomings, not the horse's. Also the horse's mouth may be sore, his teeth may need filing, he may have a bad tooth or sore cheeks or even damaged bars to the mouth. Make sure that there is no other reason for the horse pulling or resisting before trying a more severe bit.

NECKSTRAP

A vital aid for beginners is a neckstrap which they can catch hold of to help them keep their balance. It is a leather strap which goes around the horse's neck – a stirrup leather can be used if nothing else is available.

THE SADDLE

The important factor about the saddle is that it is comfortable for both horse and rider. A good saddle which is the correct size helps the rider to sit in the right position, so beginners should take expert

26 (*Above*) A jumping saddle.
27 (*Below*) A dressage saddle

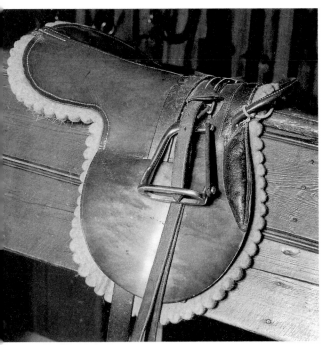

25 A child's saddle for early learning with a handle for support and safety stirrups

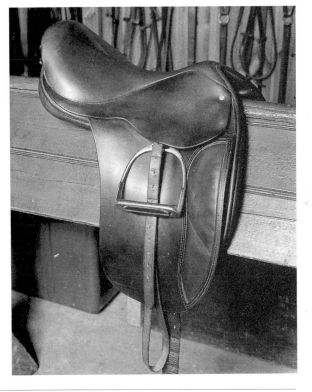

advice when buying this important item of equipment.

The general purpose saddle is the best type for beginners. It is only when you start to concentrate on a discipline that a specialist saddle is needed: either the straighter flapped, deep-seated dressage saddle, or the longer seated, forward-cut jumping saddle, or the very light, very forward-cut racing saddle. For young children a felt saddle is most comfortable and less slippery. The majority of felt saddles have a strap at the front which children can hold to help them to balance.

The parts of a saddle

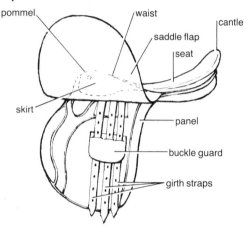

A saddle is made up of a number of sections. The tree determines the shape (i.e. general purpose, dressage, etc.). The pommel is the front of the saddle and must be high and wide enough to clear the horse's withers; the cantle is the back of the saddle; the panel is the padding separating the tree from the horse; the knee rolls help to keep the rider's legs in place; the seat affects the rider's position and can be deep, shallow, narrow or broad; the saddle flaps can be forward cut for jumping or relatively straight for dressage or showing; the stirrup bars hold the stirrup leathers; the straps hold the girth, and should be fitted with buckle guards to prevent the girth buckles from damaging the saddle flaps; sweat flaps separate the girth straps from the horse.

Separate from the saddle is the girth which can be string, webbing or leather. Whichever material is chosen, it must be of good quality because it is always very dangerous if a girth breaks.

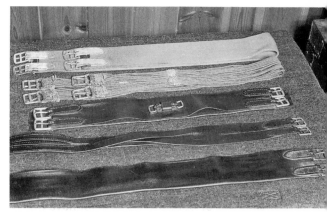

28 Various girths. *From top to bottom:* web girth, string girth, short three-fold dressage girth, leather Balding girth, long three-fold leather girth

STIRRUP IRONS AND LEATHERS

Attached to the stirrup bars are the stirrup leathers and irons. The latter must be wide enough for the rider's foot to slide out easily. If the iron is so small that the foot touches both sides at the same time, it is easy for the foot to be caught up in the event of a fall, and the rider will then be dragged along. Children may use safety stirrups, which have a detachable thick rubber band on one side rather than solid metal.

29 A safety stirrup with detachable rubber band

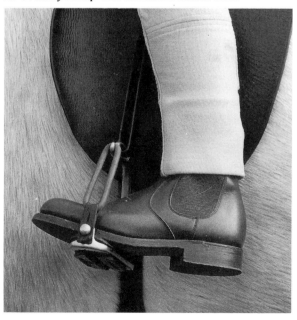

NUMNAH

A numnah is used to prevent sweat getting into the saddle and to soften the contact between the saddle and the horse. It can be made of a wide range of materials, the important factors being that it fits and does not wrinkle under the saddle; that it is securely attached to the saddle or girth so it does not slide back; and that it is regularly cleaned to prevent yesterday's dirt being rubbed into the horse's back.

CRUPPER AND BREASTPLATE

Some horses' or ponies' backs do not have a good saddle position, with the result that the saddle tends to slip forwards or backwards. A crupper can be used to stop it slipping forwards and a breastplate to prevent it moving backwards. Both the crupper and breastplate should be fitted so that they are not in play when the saddle is in its correct position. Only if the saddle slips forward should the crupper tighten and so stop it, and the same applies to the breastplate in the case of a saddle which slides back.

MARTINGALES

Martingales can be used with horses who put their heads in the air. The standing martingale runs from the girth to the back of the noseband and is particularly useful with beginners, as the horse can only resist against this strap rather than pulling the reins. The running martingale is also fitted to the girth, but ends in two rings through which the reins run. When coming into action it affects the rein pressure. The correct length is when the rings can reach to the thoat. For the beginner a standing martingale is usually most suitable, as it will be difficult for him to keep the constant contact with the mouth needed for the running martingale to be effective. For more experienced riders I prefer running martingales as one can feel and to some extent control their influence over the horse.

All auxiliary tack – martingales, the various nosebands, cruppers and breastplates – can be used to fix a problem. If the horse opens his mouth, use a drop noseband; if he crosses his jaw, then try a Grakle or a flash noseband; if he puts his head in the air, use a martingale; but do not put on these extra bits of leather unless they are necessary. Do not use them simply because they look smart.

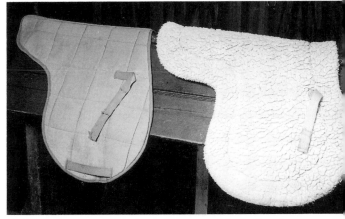

30 Washable numnahs – for a dressage saddle (*left*) and for a jumping saddle (*right*)

31 Horse wearing a running martingale

32 Horse wearing a standing martingale attached to a cavesson noseband

BOOTS AND BANDAGES

Boots are used to protect the horse's legs, bandages to protect and support. I use boots as a precaution against blows and strains, but they are rarely necessary when beginners are doing straightforward work or riding a horse who does not 'move close' or hit his legs (check to see if there are marks on the inside of the legs and, if there are, fit a pair of boots to protect that part of the leg). Brushing boots are used to protect the lower limbs from below the knee to the fetlock joints. Overreach boots protect the coronet and heels from blows from the hind feet; injuries which usually only occur when jumping. These and Yorkshire boots are used to protect the inner sides of the hind fetlocks. Polo boots protect the whole leg including the pasterns.

It is important that boots should fit well and be carefully adjusted: neither so tight that they damage the shin joints or tendons, nor so loose that they rub or slip down. The application of bandages is discussed in Chapter 12 under Stable Duties.

CARE OF TACK

All tack should be cleaned and checked after use to keep it in good condition and reduce the risk of breaks and tears. Bandages and numnahs need washing and drying at regular intervals. Metal parts need cleaning with a damp cloth, then drying; rubber, plastic and suede should be cleaned with a damp cloth or sponge, as should all leather. Leather is then soaped or, occasionally, oiled. In Chapter 16 there is a more detailed account about looking after equipment.

PUTTING ON THE SADDLE

Before putting on the tack, tie the horse up in his headcollar. The saddle is carried to the horse with the stirrup irons run up (see photograph 33).

The horse's saddle is put on (see photographs 34–36) from the near (left) side, and lifted on to rest just above the withers before being gently pushed back until it sits in the deepest part of the horse's back.

If a numnah is being used, put this on before the saddle, and when the saddle is placed on top of it ensure that the numnah is pulled up into the pommel and is not pressed down across the top of the

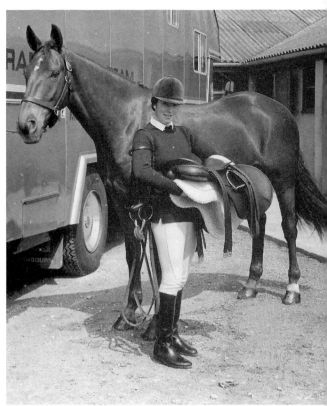

33 How to carry the saddle and bridle

withers by the saddle. The girth is then slid down and checked for straightness before being done up on the near side. The girth should be gradually tightened and with a tense horse it helps to lead him forward a few steps to get him more relaxed before each tightening. When the girth is fully tightened the buckles should be level on both sides.

FITTING THE SADDLE

It is important to check the fit of the saddle as it is all too easy to give a horse a saddle sore, especially in the wither area. Over the withers it should be high and wide enough not to pinch. It should be possible to put three fingers between the pommel and the horse when nobody is sitting in the saddle. It is also important that the seat rests securely on the horse's back and that the rear of the saddle is not so much above the horse that it will move from side to side and rub his back, or so low or narrow that it comes into contact with the backbone.

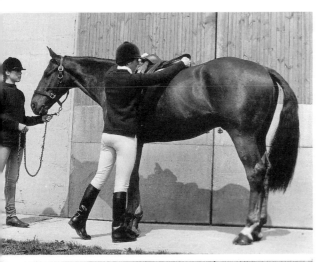

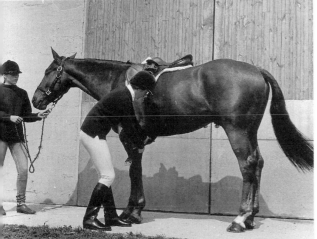

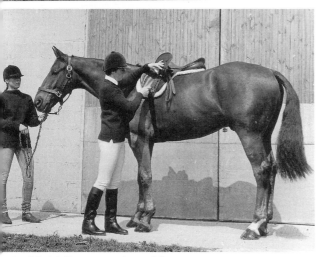

34–36 Putting on the saddle

PUTTING ON THE BRIDLE

To put on the bridle first hold it (as shown in photographs 37–43) at the headpiece in the left hand. As with the saddle, approach the horse on the nearside, then stand alongside the neck, facing forwards. Put the right arm around the off-side of his head so that the hand rests on his nasal bones. Unfasten the headcollar rope from the headcollar or from the tying up ring. Slip the reins over his head with the right hand, undo and take off the headcollar and then return the hand to hold his face. Put the cheekpieces of the bridle into the right hand. Slip the bit into his mouth with the left hand, if necessary gently encouraging him to open his jaw by pushing the left thumb between his lips where there is a gap between his teeth, and at the same time slowly lift the bridle with the right. When he opens his mouth take the headpiece in the left hand and slip it over his ears. The right hand can be used to push the ears under the headpiece. Fasten the throatlash and the noseband.

TAKING OFF THE SADDLE

To take off the saddle, the stirrups are run up, the reins taken over the horse's head and held, while the girth is undone and the pommel taken with the left hand; the saddle is then lifted away from the horse towards the person, and the left hand slipped under the arch. The right hand is used to catch the girth and hook it over the seat.

TAKING OFF THE BRIDLE

To take off the bridle, unfasten the throatlash and noseband. Stand in the same position as when putting it on and slip the reins up to the headpiece. Fasten the headcollar around his neck, then with a hand on either side take hold of the browband and push it forwards so that the headpiece slips over the ears. When, and only when, free of the ears, gradually lower the bridle so that the bit slips out of the horse's mouth. Put on the headcollar while holding the headpiece of the bridle in the left hand.

FITTING THE BRIDLE

The fit of the bridle is very important (see photographs 41 and 43). The throatlash should be loose

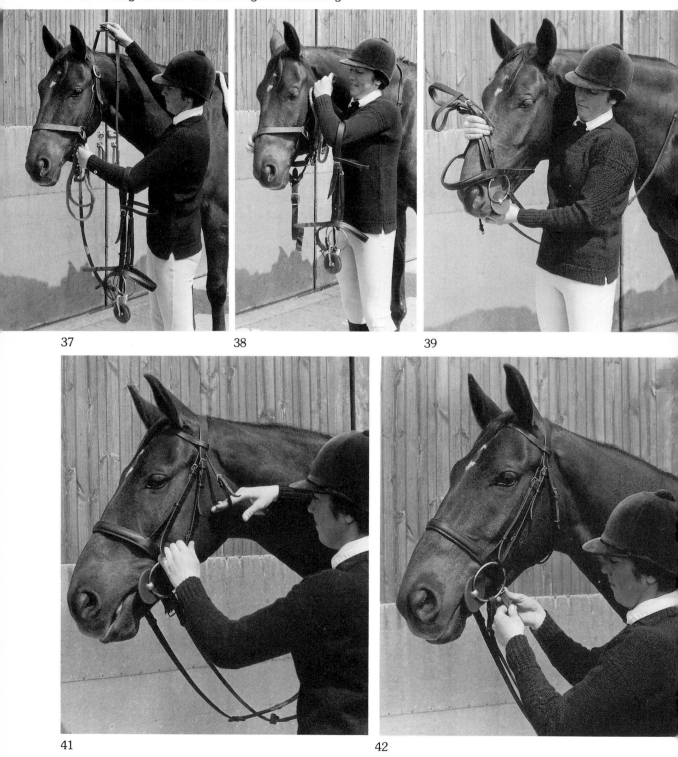

37

38

39

41

42

40

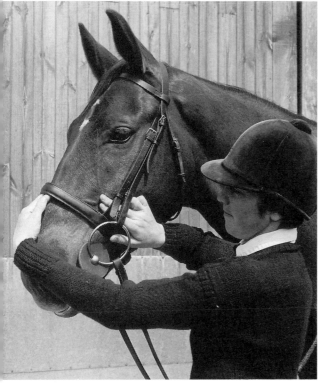

43

enough to allow you to put four fingers between it and the horse. The browband should not be too short otherwise it will rub the ears, nor so long that it droops. The cavesson noseband should be high enough for the skin not to get pinched between it and the bit, when the bit comes into play. It should lie about two fingers' width below the protruding jawbone. It is normal to tighten the cavesson noseband until one finger can be placed between it and the horse, though with a horse who consistently opens his mouth it can be tightened further.

A drop noseband, by tightening over the nostrils, can easily restrict the horse's breathing. To prevent this it should be fitted about four fingers' width above the nostrils at the front and in the chin groove behind. The front piece must be short enough for its cheekpieces to be well in front of the horse's lips, otherwise it will pinch the lips around the bit.

The Grakle noseband is usually bought without a pin or stitching fixing the join between the upper and lower straps. This pin should be fixed in such a position that there is a good range of adjustments to the noseband, i.e. when done up normally both straps should fasten at the middle hole. The cheekpieces should reach to just below the cheekbones. The top strap should be done up tightly and the bottom with enough room to put two fingers through it.

The bit must be of the correct width for the horse's mouth (see photograph 21). If it is too wide, it will hang low in the mouth, making it easy for the horse to get his tongue over it. If it is too narrow, it will make the mouth sore by pinching the inside of the cheeks against his teeth. When pulled straight in the horse's mouth, about $\frac{1}{4}$ in. of the bit should be seen on either side.

The height of the bit in the mouth is adjusted by the buckles on the bridle cheekstraps so that it just wrinkles the corners of the mouth.

With curb bits the curb chain should be attached to the hook on the offside, turned clockwise to lie flat and then hooked into the curb chain hook on the nearside. The surplus links should hang down, divided equally between the two sides, odd surplus links usually being kept on the nearside. The correctly adjusted curb chain makes contact when the cheeks of the curb are at 45° angle to the vertical. Twist the chain to lie flat against the chin, as twists can hurt the horse and make him pull harder.

4 · GETTING ON AND OFF

Before getting on the horse lead him to a suitable area which is flat and as quiet as possible.

LEADING

To lead a horse the reins are taken over his head and held with the right hand close to the bit and the left at the buckle end. The horse should not be pulled, so the leader must walk alongside the head and neck, not in front of the horse. If the horse is lazy, a whip can be carried in the left hand and used with little taps where the leg aids are given just behind the saddle. The voice can also be used, soothingly to calm or slow him down, more urgently and sharply to make him go forward. It is important not to look at the horse as this makes him stop. He is far more likely to follow you than advance towards an irate glare.

MOUNTING

At the area chosen for getting on, the reins are put back over his head. It is best that a novice finds a person to hold the head of the horse, and essential for a beginner to do so. The more experienced who are mounting on their own should put their arms through the rein when making final adjustments to tack.

The rider must double-check that the girths are tight enough, as a slipping saddle can be very dangerous. If it slips back, it will make a horse buck, if it slips sideways, the rider will be thrown. Then the length of the stirrups can be tested. The knuckles of the rider's right hand are placed level with the stirrup bar and he holds the base of the stirrup iron with his left hand. For the approximate correct length the stirrup iron should just reach his right armpit. When he is in the saddle the stirrup length can be adjusted again if the rider is not comfortable. It is important that the stirrups are not so short as to raise the knees and push the seat backwards, nor so long as to make the rider feel that he is reaching for the stirrups, leaning forward and taking his weight off his seat bones.

To get on (see photographs 44–47), the rider stands on the nearside close to the horse's shoulder and facing the hindquarters. With his left hand he takes hold of both reins and either grasps a tuft of mane near the withers or spreads his hand across the horse's neck so that he can press down and balance on it.

He holds the stirrup with the right hand and puts his left foot into it, taking care to keep the toe down so that it does not dig into the horse. His right hand is then taken across the saddle to hold the seat on the offside. He pushes off with his right foot, transferring his weight into the left stirrup; swings his right leg across and well above the quarters; slips his right hand forward, and uses both hands to balance on as he lowers himself gently into the saddle. Then he puts his right foot in the stirrup iron and takes hold of the reins with both hands.

Should a horse move when the rider is getting on it may lead to a fall so, if there is no assistant on hand, the rider should use his voice and the reins to ensure that the horse remains still.

Once the rider is in the saddle the girths can be checked again. This is usually best done after asking the horse to walk a few steps so that he has had the chance to relax his muscles and does not 'blow out' (inhale and hold his breath to resist the tightening). To adjust the girths the reins are taken in

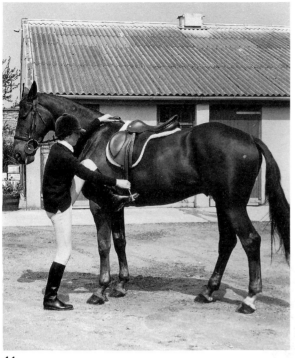

44

45

46

47

48 Checking and tightening the girths

49

one hand and the leg, with the foot still in the iron, is lifted up and forward of the saddle. The free hand is then used to raise the saddle flap and gradually tighten the girths.

DISMOUNTING

To get off (see photographs 49–51), the rider puts the reins into his left hand, which he stretches over the neck close to the withers, and puts his right hand on the right knee roll; both hands can thus be used to support the rider's weight. The rider then takes both feet out of the stirrups, leans forward and swings his right leg back clean over the horse's quarters to land with both feet on the ground facing the horse.

Riders can get off keeping the left foot in the stirrup when swinging the right across, then putting the weight on to the hands and releasing the left foot from the stirrup. I do not advocate this method as it is too easy for the left foot to get trapped in the stirrup. An even more dangerous method of getting off is swinging the right leg forwards over the horse's neck, because if the horse moves the rider can be thrown on to his back.

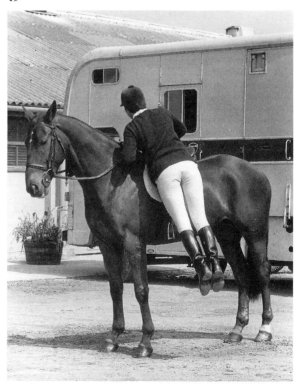

50

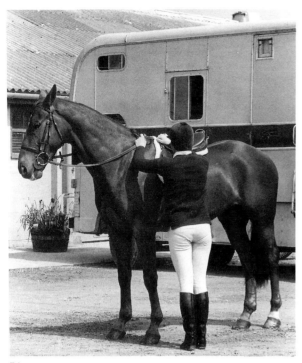

51

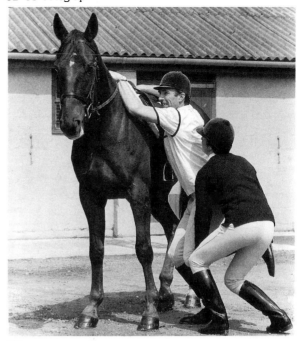

52

THE LEG-UP

A leg-up can be a useful way of mounting on nervous horses. The rider's hands are put in the usual position. The rider faces the horse and lifts his left leg which the helper can then grasp with the left hand under the knee and with the right just above the ankle. Most riders then bounce a couple of times before springing upwards as high as possible, aided by pressing down on the withers with the left hand and pulling with the right hand. The helper lifts the left leg upwards and the rider swings his right over the quarters. Then he lowers himself, as always, quietly and gradually into the saddle.

The rider must not expect the helper to do all the work. A successful leg-up is a combined effort by the rider to spring and the helper to lift.

VAULTING

I usually vault into the saddle as I have a back problem and cannot put my foot in the stirrup iron. I put my hands in the same position as when getting on normally, then take a couple of bounces which help me to jump high enough to get my arms straight. I can then swing my right leg over. The

53

secret is to jump, pull with the right arm and push with the left all at the same time! There are many other ways of vaulting on and people tend to develop a technique that suits their own physique.

54–57 Vaulting on

54

55

56

57

5 · THE POSITION

The aim is for the rider to remain still in the saddle, since any changes in the distribution of his weight inhibit the horse's action. Movement by the rider causes the horse to adjust by trying to move (usually sideways) in order to come under where the rider places most of his weight.

The rider's weight should remain in the same position in the saddle and to do this he must be balanced at all times. For the rider to stay in the same position when the horse is moving, he has to absorb the movement of the horse's back under the saddle with his own back and hips. He can only do this if he is relaxed and supple. If any part of his body stiffens he will set up a resistance against the movement of the horse, and when the horse meets that resistance its movement will not be absorbed but will shift the rider. Unable to maintain his position, the rider will tense up, grip and so cause more resistance, thus creating a vicious circle.

THE BASIC POSITION

The key to keeping the weight steady in the saddle is to be relaxed and confident enough for there to be no tension, but not so relaxed that the body is slumped: it must be kept upright and in a balanced position. The shoulder, hip and heel should be on a perpendicular line, with the weight equally divided between the two seat bones. In this position the rider is naturally balanced, just as if he were standing on the ground. He can keep in balance with his horse and needs no support, either from the reins or by gripping with the legs. This is known as the basic position (see photograph 58).

The head must be kept upright and if the rider does need to look down it should only be to glance with his eyes. If the head tips forward, it brings the body forward and the balanced position is lost. When riding it is important to feel proud and to be able to say, 'Look at me, I am the smartest thing that ever sat on a horse.'

The position of the shoulders contributes towards this proud attitude. They must not be rounded, but should be kept back, like the head, so that the rider's upper body is upright and straight. The back should be erect, neither slumped nor hollow, and positioned vertically above the seat bones, which bear equal amounts of the weight.

The thighs should lie flat against the saddle and as vertical as possible without lifting the seat bones. They must not grip the saddle as this leads to

58 A good basic position

tension, followed by resistance against the movement of the horse.

The legs should hang down either side of the horse without gripping, the knees resting on the saddle and the lower legs quietly on the horse's sides. All the joints – the hip, knee and ankle – should be relaxed and free to flex with the horse's movement.

The balls of the feet should rest lightly on the irons, with the weight directed into the heels so that they sink below the level of the toes. The ball of the foot should rest on the iron but not be pushed, as this makes the knee and heel come up, the body tip forward and the shoulders fall in front of the hips and heels. In this position the rider can no longer be in balance and he will tend to hold himself in position by gripping with his calves or supporting himself on his irons.

The arms should hang in a natural relaxed way by the rider's sides with the elbows over the hip bones. The lower arm and rein are kept in a straight line and the hands held just above the withers. The wrists should have a slight tendency to turn the fingers inwards, with the thumbs on top. The elbows should not move from the rider's sides. In maintaining this position there should be no tension. The fingers and wrists should be able to feel what the horse is doing and if necessary gently to move the bit in the horse's mouth without any movement of the arms.

I divide riders into two basic types – the beer drinkers and the pram or baby carriage pushers! The beer drinkers keep their wrists turned slightly to bring their fingers inwards and their thumbs on top, and can therefore feel every movement of the horse's mouth. The pram pushers, however, have the backs of their hands uppermost with their thumbs underneath and often the hands turned slightly outwards. In this position it is impossible to feel what the horse is doing and the rider will always exert a dead pull on the horse's mouth through the weight of the arm pulling backwards. This inhibits the forward movement of the horse.

Another fault is to hold the hands below the withers. This is usually done by the beginner to get the horse to lower his head. In fact it has just the opposite effect. Firstly, the rider loses his balance as his upper body tips forward when the hands are pushed down. Secondly, the angle of the rein pressure means that the bit is pulling down on the

59 This is a 'pram pusher', with the wrists horizontal and a broken line between the elbow and the bit. The rider is leaning forward, and his lower leg is too far forward

60 This rider has allowed his heel to come up and he is holding his hands too low

bars of the horse's mouth. The horse finds it very easy to set himself against this and to use all the muscle under the neck to render the rider's efforts ineffective.

The hand holds the rein, which comes from the bit, between the fourth and little finger and allows it to pass up through the palm to leave between the first finger and the thumb. The buckle end of the rein then falls on the horse's off side. The fingers should hold the rein as if it were a sponge, so that they are neither clenched nor open. In this manner there is scope to move the fingers in either direction to adjust the pressure on the reins. When there is a strong contact, to stop the reins slipping through the hands it is best to apply pressure with the thumb on the first finger rather than by tightening the fist.

That is the theory of the position, which is relatively easy to establish when the horse is standing still but harder to maintain when he starts to move.

The rider has to keep contact by means of the seat bones, legs and hands; he has to keep in balance with the horse whatever is happening. The seat bones must not leave the saddle, for then the contact and balance is lost and the rider cannot feel what is happening. Loss of seat bone contact is like breaks in radio signals: there is intermittent reception and only half the message is received.

The seat bones have to stay in the saddle and can only do so if the horse's movement is absorbed by a supple, relaxed lower back and hips, and if the rider is totally committed to going with the horse. The hands have to keep a constant contact through the reins with the bit, so that they follow any movement of the horse's head, and the legs have to stay quietly on the horse's sides. All this will not be achieved in one day and in fact takes many years to perfect, but even from day one the beginner can make a start.

WALKING

The walk is the easiest pace at which to maintain these vital contacts because there is no moment of suspension which tends to throw the rider out of the saddle. The movement is mostly on a horizontal plane, as in walk the horse always has at least two legs on the ground. The walk is the best pace in which to learn to remain in balance with the horse and can be returned to whenever balance is lost in the trot or canter.

When the horse walks the rider relaxes and follows the movement, allowing the seat bones to tip slightly and travel back and forth, but without slipping to either side.

As the horse's head nods in the walk, the rider must allow his hands and arms to follow this movement so that they go forward and back with every stride. If he keeps his hands still, one moment he will be stopping the horse, the next dropping the contact. This will mean he is not achieving the aim of maintaining a constant contact.

TROTTING

The trot is a much more difficult pace in which to maintain the position. There is a moment of suspension every time a pair of diagonal legs lifts off the ground and before the other pair returns to it. This creates considerable up-and-down movement which has to be absorbed if the seat bones are to remain in constant and even contact with the saddle.

To avoid the problem the rider can go into rising trot: he rises out of the saddle as one of the diagonal pairs leaves the ground and returns to it as the same pair comes back to the ground, and sits in the saddle for every alternate step. It is important when he rises out of the saddle that he brings his hips forward towards the pommel of the saddle while keeping his body upright, rather than lifting his whole body upwards or forwards, causing a loss of balance. He should not rise far out of the saddle and should return gently to it (see photograph 61).

The rider rises when one pair of diagonals lifts from the ground and sits as they return to it. Most people agree that when working on circles and turns balance is best achieved if the rider rises as the inside hind and outside foreleg touch the ground. He can check this by watching if the outside shoulder is the furthest forward as he rises from the saddle and the inside shoulder furthest forward as he sits. With frequent riding he will start to feel on which diagonal he is rising and whether it is the correct diagonal (i.e. rising when the inside hind and outside foreleg are forward). I in fact tend to look at the inside shoulder and check that I am sitting when the shoulder is forward.

To change diagonal the rider does a double bump, sitting for two strides and then continuing in

61 The rider in a good position at the rising trot. The body is upright and balanced, the hips are coming forward over the pommel and the seat is not lifted far out of the saddle

rising trot on the other diagonal. It is helpful to practise these changes while trotting in straight lines and it is important to change diagonals frequently when hacking otherwise the horse will become one sided from using one side of his back more than the other. I change diagonals every kilometre on the roads and tracks in a three-day event to prevent the horse becoming tired or stiff on one side.

Most riders find the sitting trot the most difficult pace in which to keep in balance. There is the up-and-down as well as the forward movement to absorb. Any stiffness in the horse's back will make the trot feel more bumpy and more difficult to sit to; any tension in the rider will make the horse stiffen against this resistance and go into a stiff, bumpy trot, so starting up a vicious circle. The rider has to relax and concentrate on keeping his seat bones in the saddle through having a rubbery tummy and lower back. The actual movement involves a slight rotation of the hips every stride, and a commitment to stay with the horse as opposed to just sit on top of him. To remain in balance in the sitting trot takes many hours of practice.

In the trot the horse's head does not nod, so the hands must remain still to maintain a constant contact.

CANTERING

The canter again involves a lifting effect, with a moment of suspension every stride, but not every step, as in the trot. Most riders find it easier to sit to, since the lift is more gradual, not so sharply up and down, and the rotation of the hips needed is more oval in shape. Again the rider needs that rubbery tummy and lower back to absorb the upward, forward and downward movement, and to ensure that the seat bones never move from the saddle. Many riders in the canter tend to rock the whole body back and forth; but it is important if balance is to be retained to take the movement with the lower back and to keep the upper body still.

In all three paces the head and shoulders should stay still. If they tip forward in front of the balanced position on the perpendicular line through the hips and heels, then the rider is forced to grip with the calves to prevent himself falling forward. As he grips, the tension shifts his balance further forward, making him grip harder.

The legs should not move involuntarily but remain by the horse's sides ready for use if needed. The hips and lower back should absorb the horse's movement but the body above and the legs below should remain still.

TURNING

To turn a corner or ride a circle the beginner has to make a conscious effort to stay in balance with the horse. He must avoid any tendency to collapse his body and drop his shoulder on one side, to fall in, as when riding a motor-bike, or to let his seat bones slip sideways (see photograph 62). He has to concentrate on keeping his body upright above that of the horse, turning his shoulders to keep them parallel with those of the horse. The seat bones should remain in the saddle; they may move backwards or forwards to help the rider keep his balance, but they must not slip to one side because then the body collapses on one side, causing a shift in the rider's weight to which the horse will have to react.

Beginners should concentrate on distributing their weight evenly on both seat bones, although more experienced riders may transfer some weight to the inside to achieve more sophisticated controls. I always approach a corner aiming to stay in balance with the horse. If I aim for that while staying relaxed, my body makes the appropriate moves to maintain my balance. I do not plan to alter my weight or position, I simply try to relax to follow the movement. If I feel I am losing my balance, I know there is some tension somewhere, so I stop the horse, roll my shoulders, swing the arms and legs, and try to become totally relaxed so that I can once again go with the horse without any need to hang on by tightening my arms or legs.

THE FORWARD SEAT

When starting to ride, and for much of the time when schooling and hacking, it is best to ride with an upright seat in the basic position as already explained. The forward seat should be used when jumping, by a beginner who is learning to canter, while warming up, or when starting to canter young horses.

62 This rider is collapsing his hip to the right so that his weight has slipped over to the left. He will not have equal weight in both seat bones

63 A good balanced turn. The rider is using his inside leg and turning his shoulders to keep them parallel with those of the horse

To use the forward seat first shorten the stirrups. It helps the beginner to establish the forward position if the horse is standing still. He should then stand up in the saddle and lean forward by bending at the ankles, knees and hips (see photograph 64).

64 The author helping a rider to find her balance in the forward seat at the halt. He is showing how the weight should fall onto the knee and the ball of the foot

65 The forward seat at the canter. The reins are a little long but the author is in a good balance

All the weight must go down through the knees on to the balls of the feet in the stirrup irons. When he has found his balance, this position can be used for cantering, although it is a useful exercise to practise the forward seat in walk and trot first.

Beginners can gain a little extra support by resting the hands on the horse's neck, but should keep checking their balance by taking the hands off the neck. If support is needed all the time then their weight is too far forward.

The lower part of the thighs and knees are used for gripping but never the calves. The movement is taken through the flexion of the hips and knees. They act as shock absorbers and, as this effect is most important, the knees should not grip too hard. They are not there primarily to take the weight but to help the rider stay in balance with the horse. Most of the weight should fall on to the balls of the feet in the stirrup irons. There should not be any weight on the seat bones, even if the seat bones might touch the saddle but even then the weight should still fall down through the knees and on to the balls of the feet.

The body is tipped forward from the hip joints and the seat bones come out of the saddle, but not so far that the rider loses balance and falls too far forward on to the neck, nor so little that he loses balance, falls back and touches the saddle with every stride.

As with the basic position, the rider can only stay in balance in the forward seat if he is not tense and lets himself go with the movement of the horse. If he stiffens, he will tip forwards and/or backwards and have to grip in order to try and stay with the horse.

In either position tension is a handicap and results in the rider's weight being shifted by the horse's movement. His balance will be lost, and only a balanced rider can keep a constant contact with his hands, seat bones and legs, and only then can he begin to develop the basis of horsemanship, which is feel.

The three keys to riding are balance, feel and co-ordination. Once the position is sufficiently established for the rider to remain in balance, then he is in a position to feel what the horse is doing, feel what is going on underneath him, so that he takes over more and more control. He takes over this control by learning to co-ordinate his means of control: the aids of the legs, seat and hands.

6 · THE AIDS

The aids are the actions taken to make the horse do what the rider wants. They have evolved over the centuries to become generally accepted as the best means of controlling the horse. It was discovered, for instance, that the best way of making the horse go forward was to kick him, rather than just to let go the reins.

The aim is to make the aids light and barely perceptible. This takes time and to achieve it the horse needs to respond freely and obediently to the aids, and the rider must have control over his position.

There are a number of aids, divided into natural aids – the hands, legs and seat, and the artificial aids – the spurs and whip.

THE HANDS

The beginner thinks of the hands as the hand brake, but it is not quite as simple as that. The hands also help the horse's balance, flexion and outline, and in practice they are not very effective at stopping the horse if the rider merely pulls back on the reins. For the best control they need to be co-ordinated with the legs and seat.

The hands are attached by the reins to a lump of steel which is in one of the tenderest parts of the horse's anatomy, its mouth. The rider must be gentle with his hands. He should, where possible, only move the fingers and not the hand, wrist and arm. If this is not effective, he should move the bit by flexing the wrists, and only as a last resort use the arms. Pulling at the horse is a natural reaction and one of the most common faults amongst beginners, but the usual result is to make the horse shorten his neck rather than slow down. Since the

66 The hands in a good position to apply the aids with the thumbs on top. The fingers are not clenched and the hands, wrists and arms are relaxed

67 Hands in the 'pram pusher' position

horse is much stronger than the rider, a tug of war is best avoided and giving and taking with the reins will be a lot more effective.

The hands can be used passively – to restrain, to give, and to feel what is happening. Most of the time they are passive and the fingers are only used to maintain a soft, elastic, positive contact with the horse's mouth, a contact which is as even as possible on both sides of the bit.

The beginner should start by riding with a pair of hands which are still and which maintain an even as possible contact with both sides of the bit. This is best achieved by keeping the hands quite close together. Those who find that their hands drift apart should practise riding with their knuckles touching.

When the horse makes a turn, beginners should endeavour to keep an even weight of contact in both hands, though more advanced riders distinguish between the outside and inside hands. The outside rein is used for support by maintaining a positive constant contact – it helps to balance the horse and regulate the pace. The inside rein is used to establish the bend by providing a light contact which encourages the horse to relax his jaw.

THE LEGS

The beginner thinks of the legs in terms of an accelerator, generating the forward momentum, but they are also directional guides which help to keep the horse straight, bent or moving sideways.

The legs can be applied close to the girth (see photograph 68), which is the nearest they come to being an accelerator, encouraging forward movement. If applied individually by the girth they also help to control the shoulders by stopping them from falling in or out around corners. When applied further behind the girth (see photograph 69) the legs control the hindquarters; and when applied individually they provide a means of asking the horse to step sideways away from the leg or of stopping the hindquarters from falling out.

68 Leg applied by the girth, but a little too far forward except when controlling the shoulder

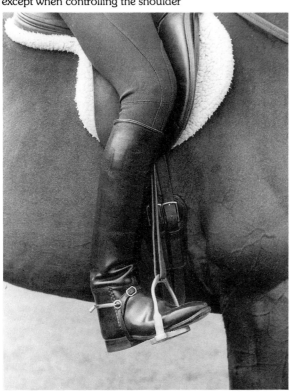

69 Leg applied behind the girth. For the canter strike off and lateral work it will need to be even further back

In controlling the shoulders or the hindquarters the legs play a supporting role and remain relatively still against the sides of the horse. As an accelerator or when asking for lateral steps they are used more actively, to give nudges, taps or kicks, depending on the response of the horse. It is important that the aids are not applied by tightening or squeezing the legs, as this creates tension in the rider's body and tends to shift him out of the saddle, so that his balance is lost. Also the horse does not react much to a constant leg pressure, but is far more responsive to a vibrating pressure or intermittent kicks.

THE SEAT

Beginners should concentrate on acquiring a balanced position and mastering the leg and hand aids before tackling those of the seat. These are made through weight adjustments by sitting heavier, lighter or by increasing the weight on one or other seat bone.

By sitting heavier the rider should increase the activity, as the horse tends to bring his hindquarters (the source of activity) further underneath his body to support this weight. The effect can be negative if the horse hollows his back against the weight of the rider, as this will push the hindquarters further out and reduce activity. To avoid the risk of producing this negative effect it is best not to use the seat as a driving/pushing aid until a rider is supple and balanced. Nor should it be used with the novice horse, who must first become sufficiently supple and muscled up along his back for the seat aids to be effective.

Beginners should aim to keep their weight evenly divided between the two seat bones. If the weight is transferred more on to one side than the other, the horse moves under the heavier side as he tends to try to catch the weight. Until a rider is sufficiently advanced to be in full control of these weight transfers, and is able to achieve them without disturbing his position and balance, it is best to aim to keep the weight even on both seat bones.

THE WHIP

The whip and spurs are called artificial aids. The whip is used to reinforce the leg aids and to teach the horse to become more responsive to the leg aids.

70 This rider is using his seat as a driving aid

When the leg aids do not produce the required result, the leg and whip can be used together just behind the girth. The next time, the leg alone is used, but because the horse associates the leg with the whip he tends to move more freely away from the leg. It is important that the rider does not pull back with the hand or catch the horse in the mouth as he uses the whip (in other words he does not apply the accelerator and hand brake at the same time). The schooling or dressage whip is applied by bringing the whip hand out to the side and twisting the wrist, and the short whip by taking the whip hand off the rein. In this way you don't hit yourself on the thigh.

The long schooling whip is used when training on the flat to reinforce the leg aids. It is applied as close as possible behind the rider's leg, starting with a tap and, if this is not effective, getting a little stronger until there is a response. As soon as the horse responds as required, pat him and say thank you, so that riding does not become a continuous chastisement.

The short whip can be used on the shoulder to help the beginner keep the horse straight approaching a fence, or if a horse shies, or by a child to encourage the pony to go forward. In the latter case it is more of a threat than an aid.

On the rare occasions that the horse is deliberately disobedient it may be necessary to use the whip as a punishment. Beginners, however, should remember that they might have caused the disobedience, as their aids are rarely clear and the horse might have found them difficult to understand. Only experienced riders should use the whip as a punishment.

To punish the horse effectively with the whip is very difficult. Most people let go the reins as they hit the horse, which simply makes the horse go faster and escape the rider's control. To be effective, the reins must be held and the reprimand given immediately the horse disobeys. The horse must associate the punishment with the crime. It is ineffective five minutes or even thirty seconds later. Once the moment is past it is too late to hit a horse and will do more harm than good. The horse will not realize why he has been reprimanded and is likely to become tense and worried.

To transfer a short whip from one hand to the other, hold both reins and the whip in one hand; with the other hand carefully pull the whip upwards until it is free and then take the rein back.

A longer whip has to be carefully swung through 180 degrees in front of the rider's face. To do this both reins are again held in the whip hand and the wrist turned so that the long end of the whip is swung gently upwards. The free hand takes hold of the whip just below the other hand and with the back of the hand towards the rider's body so that it will be held correctly when it returns to its basic position. This is done by swinging the whip through the remainder of the arc, the other hand having let go of the whip. The new whip hand then retakes its rein.

SPURS

Spurs are used to increase the horse's response to the leg aid but, like the whip, must be used cautiously. Spurs should not be worn until a rider is in control of his balance and seat, because only then can he use the spurs when they are needed and not inadvertently catch the horse.

To apply the spur the toe is turned out slightly and the spur brought into contact with the horse. Riders should not try to use the spur every stride as the horse then becomes 'dead' to the spur; nor should the rider raise his heel to try and make contact with the horse, as this will tend to make him lose his balance.

VOICE

The voice is very important because horses respond to it as a means of encouragement, reward and admonishment. The horse can become very responsive to it. If when patting a horse the rider also says 'good boy', the tone of voice helps the horse to relax and appreciate that he has done the right thing. Horses soon learn to associate a click with the need to go faster and a growl or sharp, distinctive tone with having done something wrong.

The highly strung horse is often made calmer by use of the voice. Muttering can help to make him relax.

When going across country it helps to have a horse who slows up when the rider says 'whoa', as this means that less restraining aids are needed, and who goes forward when the rider growls at him, especially if there is a difficult fence ahead.

CO-ORDINATION OF AIDS

Once you have understood the individual aids, remember that the art of riding is in combining and co-ordinating them. I cannot think of any instruction to a horse which does not entail use of at least two of the three natural aids.

To go forward

From a halt to go forward into a walk nudge (if necessary tap or kick) with the legs by the girth and

71 In using the spur to reinforce the leg aids this rider's heel has come up, as has the knee, which will tend to tip the upper body forward. Instead the toes should have been turned out to use this artificial aid

allow with the hands, but only by softening the contact, not by letting it go. As the horse starts to move, the rider must be relaxed enough to follow the movement with his seat bones and also with his hands.

In all forward transitions the principle is similar: additional leg, allowing and softening with the hands, and the readiness of the seat to follow the movement.

As the canter can be on either lead, slightly different aids are needed to ensure that the horse starts on the required leg. The inside leg is applied by the girth to act as an accelerator and the outside leg is brushed back along the horse's side to indicate that the outside hind should start the canter sequence. The inside knee is pushed slightly forward which brings the inside seat bone slightly forward and the weight slightly to that side. The horse will want to bring the inside hind further forward on that side in order to catch the weight and so will tend to strike off on the required lead. At the same time the rein aids are adjusted so that there is a slight flexion to the inside; the inside rein asks for this by taking and giving, and the outside rein controls the amount of flexion and the speed of the horse.

The rein aids and the inside leg prepare the horse for the strike off; the outside leg and the transfer of weight on to the seat bone which has been pushed forward are applied at the moment the canter is required. The rider must then be ready to follow the movement of the new pace with his seat.

The beginner should learn to get his horse to strike off on the required lead by starting on a corner (so that the horse or pony is more easily flexed to the inside), and should concentrate on brushing his outside leg back and applying his inside leg by the girth. As he becomes more competent in the use of these simple canter aids, he can begin to think about the other aids (the hands and seat) so that he can get his horse on to the required lead wherever he chooses and not just at the easy spot when turning a corner.

To reduce speed

In moments of dire stress riders may have to pull on the reins to reduce speed, but this is not the way to train a horse. Just as the beginner starts by kicking to go forward, he simply pulls to stop; but as he develops his seat, balance and feel he can co-ordinate his aids to produce much more effective results. Pulling on the reins, although instinctive, must be avoided, since the horse will simply shorten his neck and hollow his back which will cause the hindquarters to fall further behind.

The aim is to contain the forward movement by restraining, not by pulling back with the hands. The rider applies his seat and legs, but because of the restraining action of the hands the horse will not go faster, but will bring his hindquarters further underneath, producing more rein pressure, which he will feel in his mouth and which will make him change down a gear. It is vital that this increased pressure on the reins is the result of the push from the seat and legs and not a pull by the hands, otherwise the horse will shorten his neck rather than bring his hindquarters underneath him.

The aids for all downward transitions are the same; it is simply a matter of the strength of the aids and their timing as to how many gears are changed down, i.e. from canter to trot or from canter to walk. With the novice horse, however, it will take more time to establish the new gear than with one who is trained (see Chapter 9).

The aim should be to keep the hands still and to push the horse with the seat and legs into that contact, providing the horse maintains a consistent contact. If he tries to escape the contact by putting his head up, poking his nose out, stiffening his back, or leaning on the bit, then move the bit in his mouth by playing with the fingers, at the same time as asking for the transition. In this way the horse will have more difficulty in catching hold of and setting against the bit.

RESPONSIVENESS

It is fundamental to riding that a horse responds. The first stages of training, for both horse and rider, cannot involve learning about co-ordinated aids; they are simply concerned with the fact that when the leg is applied the horse goes forward and when the rein is used he stops or turns. Fundamental to the use of co-ordinated aids is that the horse goes freely forward as soon as the leg aids are applied. He has to go forward without being thumped every stride. He has to be responsive if the rider is to use his co-ordinated aids effectively. This is discussed further in Chapter 9.

7·FIRST LESSONS

THE LEARNING PROCESS

There are ways of helping the learning process. As in other sports, try to store in the mind a picture of good moments and good feelings, then when your riding is not going well think back to those moments, remember how success was achieved, what it felt like, and try to aim for it again.

Those who want to be successful riders must be self-critical and cannot simply accept whatever is achieved. If second best is accepted then that becomes par and the rider will only be second best. If a movement or transition does not work, or the rider has a problem, he should not accept it but should go on working at it until it starts to improve and eventually comes right; then the good ways will become habits and your riding will improve. I keep making mistakes, but every time I make a mistake I stop, work out what I did wrong, decide what I have to do to get it right and try it again; if it is better, not necessarily perfect, I am usually satisfied; if it is wrong, I try something different.

The first stage is to stop and work out what is going wrong. Carrying on regardless rarely produces a solution. If, for instance, you start to bump around in the saddle, stop, think and analyse. Ask such questions as, 'Am I tight in my back?', 'Am I sitting up?', 'Am I in balance?', etc. It does not matter what the standard of the rider is, everybody has this kind of problem; I find it best to stop, think, let go, and start again after I have identified the cause. This disciplined process is the key to progress.

The best aid to learning at all stages, up to Grand Prix dressage or jumping, is to ride a horse who

already knows what the rider is being taught. Once the rider has felt what is needed he can work towards the same feel on other horses or ponies.

As a boy I was lucky enough to have three ponies at different times who all knew their job; all I had to do was sit and steer. They taught me to ride and made my riding fun. After learning from them I could take on younger horses and train them. When I started show jumping at international level I was given the ride on the experienced and successful horse Hideaway. He was a wonderful schoolmaster and gave me the most tremendous help when I was learning about this form of jumping, which demands so much more precision than in horse trials. The easiest way to learn is through the experiences gained on a horse who knows the work rather than by being told what to do. Teachers can talk about feel, balance and rhythm but such things are all myths until they have been experienced.

If possible learn to press the buttons on an educated horse, an older pony or a retired competition horse.

THE FIRST STEPS

The first time on horseback it is best for the beginner to be led and it is usual to do this from the left side. The leading rein is put through the left snaffle ring and attached to the ring on the other side. For a child it is best to have two people, one to look after the pony and the other the child.

Until the beginner gets balanced he can hold on to the neck strap or, if there is one, the handle at the front of the saddle. Before starting to walk around allow the beginner to become familiar with the pieces of equipment, sitting in the saddle, hold-

72 *Left:* The author on his great 'schoolmaster', Hideaway

The first difficult stage is to master the rising trot and the leader can help by saying, 'up, down, up, down,' in the rhythm of the stride. The beginner needs some help to keep his balance. If he uses the reins, he stops the horse and/or jerks him in the mouth, so it is vital that he holds on to a strap until he learns the feel of the rising trot.

Except with small ponies. who cannot go very fast, it is difficult to lead the beginner at the canter, so he must have become reasonably balanced and in control of the horse or pony before trying this pace. It is advisable that the first canters are in a confined space in case braking becomes a problem.

It is sometimes easier to learn to keep balanced in the canter by riding in the forward seat rather than the basic position. Children often find it difficult to absorb the movement when sitting in the saddle and keep their balance better in a forward seat.

LEADING FROM ANOTHER HORSE

Those who have learnt to trot and canter in an enclosed space and want to make their first ventures into the open may be led from another horse. However, this is safe only if the leader is a competent rider, and if he is on a horse with a quiet temperament who has first had a practice session leading a pony without a novice rider. With these qualifications it is a valuable exercise, especially for children, who will have fun and find it easier to do the faster paces. Also rides can start to be longer, more interesting and varied with some of the thrills of riding experienced for the first time.

LUNGEING AND WORK WITHOUT STIRRUPS

Lungeing can be a useful if sometimes painful exercise, particularly for riders who lack balance. An enclosed space, a comfortable, quiet horse and a competent, experienced lunger are the essential requirements. If these provisos can be met, then five- or ten-minute lungeing sessions, especially at the beginning of a lesson, can help the rider enormously to get the feel of keeping his balance, going with the horse and concentrating on his position without having to worry about the controls.

Work without stirrups is helpful both on and off the lunge, but it is best to hold a strap or the pommel of the saddle to start with, until the rider

73–74 Learning to rise to the trot. Note the use of the extra rein to stop the pony snatching the rein and eating grass

ing the reins and keeping the feet in the irons. Then, once used to walking and changing direction, try the occasional halt to get him used to stopping and starting. This is probably enough for the first day, because everybody is nervous and tense when they first start and therefore tend to get tired very quickly.

75 Learning to canter in the forward seat

76 Loosening up by riding without stirrups

is confident enough to relax and stay balanced. For young children the sessions must be short, but adults are stronger and should be able to cope with longer periods. The more relaxed the rider becomes the longer the session can be. If the rider gets tense, he will tire easily.

With stirrups the temptation is to put too much weight on the balls of the feet, which pushes the rider out of the saddle, lightening the amount of weight on the seat bones. If the rider is not sufficiently relaxed to follow the movements of the horse, then this is an easy way of avoiding having to absorb the movement, but it is not a balanced position nor is it the best one for controlling the horse. Without stirrups there is no escape: the rider has to stay on his seat bones.

Some days, when I am stiff and cannot sit in the saddle, I do work without stirrups. Even as riders progress, five- or ten-minute sessions without stirrups are useful to establish a balanced, relaxed position. Many great riders make this a daily exercise, but it is better first to loosen up the horse in rising trot to ensure his back is not stiff. A stiff back jolts even the most supple rider and makes sitting trot very uncomfortable.

When starting to trot without stirrups it is best to begin in a slow jog so that the rider does not have to absorb the greater movement of the longer, faster strides. A beginner, until he is confident enough to relax, can catch hold of the pommel or a strap to stop himself being bounced out of the saddle. Once a rider becomes tense it is difficult to relax again, so if this happens it is best to go back to the walk, swing the arms and legs, get relaxed and start again. As soon as the rider tenses his muscles he will be shifted in the saddle. It is important to avoid creating this tension, so use the strap or pommel to balance on. Do not try a stronger trot than is possible to sit to easily, and as soon as the tension appears, return to the walk and start again.

EXTRA CONTROLS

Ponies often try to stop and eat grass, especially when ridden by children who are weak or inexperienced. A piece of string from the saddle through the browband to the bit, or from the saddle straight to the bit, stops them boring their way to the ground and all too often chucking the child over their heads (see photograph 73).

EXERCISES

Exercises help to improve a rider's suppleness and balance, as well as his confidence on and around the horse, and they can be fun.

They can be done either when the horse or pony is stationary or while being lunged at walk or trot, and except for nervous beginners they are most effective if done without stirrups. It is best to start when the horse is stationary and being held. Then, as the rider becomes more competent, progress to trying them when walking on the lunge and then trotting.

The following are useful:

- Shoulder shrugging: the shoulders are raised as high as possible towards the ears and then dropped down again.
- Rotating the arms forward, sideways and backwards (see photograph 78).
- Bending the upper body forwards and downwards and then backwards (but only with someone holding the horse or pony).
- Touching the toes (see photograph 77).
- Stretching both legs as far backwards as possible.
- Scissors: the legs are straightened and swung alternately, one leg back and the other forwards, but all the time keeping the seat bones in the saddle.
- Jockey position: holding the front of the saddle, the rider leans forward and draws the legs up into a racing position (no stirrups).
- Ankle exercise: the ankles are turned in as full a circle as possible, first clockwise then anticlockwise.
- Vaulting on and off.
- Round the world: the right leg is lifted over the horse's neck so that the rider sits as if riding side-saddle; the left leg is swung over the hindquarters and the rider faces backwards; then the right leg is swung over, to sit side-saddle; and finally the left leg is brought over the neck, returning the rider to the normal position. This can be done clockwise, too. The pony must be held by an assistant for this exercise (see photograph 79).

77 The exercise of touching the toes

78 *Top:* The exercise of swinging the arms clockwise then anticlockwise

79 *Above:* Round the world exercise

GETTING FIT

The best way of getting fit for riding is to ride as much as possible. Different muscles are used from those in other sports. I used to be very fit at school, playing rugger and taking part in athletics, but after my first ride in the holidays I was as stiff as a board the next day.

On the other hand, increasing the general level of fitness might not develop the riding muscles but it does have other benefits. The brain takes 80 per cent of the oxygen which enters the body. When muscles tire they require a greater proportion of this oxygen. Therefore, the brain receives less, which makes it more difficult to concentrate, remain alert and maintain a balanced position on the horse. It is then that mistakes are made and accidents sometimes happen. So for those who are not fit, although riding can still be enjoyable, it will be more difficult to remain in control and to get the best out of the horse.

Skipping, sit-ups, squats and squeezing a ball in the palm of the hand all help a rider to handle himself better. Even looking after the horses helps raise the general fitness level.

As suppleness is such a crucial part of good riding, some people practise stretching exercises before getting on the horse.

HACKING OUT

Learning to ride should be fun and hacking out is one way of making it so. Riders can see more of the country as they are high enough to look over the hedges. Also they seem to be less frightening to birds and animals, who will come much closer to them than they will to people on foot or in a car.

Beginners should only go out with someone else; in fact, all riders should try to avoid hacking out alone. Then in the event of an accident there is another rider to help or go for assistance.

Apart from providing enjoyment of the country, hacking can be used to consolidate earlier lessons and as a continuation of a schooling session. Stirrups can be taken away or exercises can be done,

80 Hacking out. It is always best to go in company if possible

such as trotting along standing up in the stirrups without sitting. This helps to develop the forward seat and the rider's balance, and at the same time strengthens the legs. A sense of balance can also be developed by riding up and down hills and over rough country. A sense of anticipation as to how to control the horse is developed through such incidents as a big lorry coming down the road or a bird flying out of the hedge. Riding outside is a wonderful way of becoming a more balanced and alert rider.

ROAD SAFETY

Accidents happen all too easily on roads. Riders must study the Highway Code, or local driving regulations, and a copy of their country's code for riding (in Britain, *Ride and Drive Safely*, published by the British Horse Society).

The most important point is that the horse or pony must be under control. If he is traffic shy, keep to minor roads and always go out with another more reliable horse and rider.

Remember to smile and thank a driver who slows down. The driver will remember this and is more likely to be considerate when he next meets horses.

On British roads riders must keep to the left, and it is forbidden to ride on footpaths or pavements, though grass (not ornamental) verges can be used where they exist.

If a car approaches from behind, it is best to keep in the road, if necessary slowing the vehicle down by waving your hand up and down, and then as the car draws near move further into the side.

The most frightening thing for most horses is when a big truck or coach suddenly overtakes from behind. When you know one is approaching, flex the horse slightly to the right so that he can see it and keep your right leg on to stop his quarters swinging out. If the horse becomes very frightened, trot on and find a gap, path or driveway, where you can get off the road and allow the vehicle past.

When there is more than one horse, then ride in pairs and if one animal is nervous or the rider inexperienced, he should stay on the inside. In heavy traffic or if a car wants to overtake on a narrow road, keep in single file, with the more experienced horse/rider closest to the oncoming vehicle.

If possible, avoid riding at night; when you are forced to do so, wear reflective (not fluorescent) materials, and fix a light on your right stirrup, or carry it, showing white to the front and red to the rear.

If a horse has to be led along the road, then keep him on the inside.

Finally, another reminder about hard hats. They should be worn at all times when riding, but are particularly important on the roads.

81 Suitably equipped for riding at night

8 · LEARNING TO JUMP

The horse should approach a fence in much the same way as a person would jump a log on his own two feet: he needs to be balanced and to run towards it with medium-length strides. If the strides are too long, it is difficult to get into the air; if they are too short, it is hard to maintain balance and momentum. It is the same with a horse, since if he takes long strides he will jump very flat and if he takes restricted ones he can only buck over the fence.

THE GOLDEN RULES

My golden rules for jumping are that the horse approaches the fence going forward with impulsion, in balance and therefore with rhythm, and that the rider waits for the fence to come to him.

Going forward

Going forward with impulsion is best thought of as the horse having power; impulsion is usually

82 Jumping can begin on the leading rein as long as the fences are very small. The saddle strap can be held to help keep the balance

defined as contained forward momentum. Many riders muddle going forward with speed and try to make their horses go faster, but this will rarely produce more power unless it is contained speed. Power only comes as the horse puts his hind legs further under his body, which happens if he tries to take faster or bigger strides but is contained by the rider's hands so that he becomes more compressed, like a spring. Impulsion, power or energy is maintained by the rider's legs and contained within the horse by the rider's hands.

It is easier to develop this impulsion if the horse has the desire to go forward and to go faster. Then the action of the rider in containing the horse to the required speed creates the power and impulsion needed by the horse to jump the fence. As the rider contains the speed so the horse will become more compressed, with the hind legs further under him, so that he will have the power and impulsion without going faster.

It is easier to develop this impulsion with a free-going horse. With a young or lazy horse the rider has to create the desire to go forward. One of the best ways, especially with the young horse, is to build up the horse's speed to faster than that needed to jump the fence in question and then, while keeping on the legs, to throttle back to the required speed.

Remember that simply making the horse go flat out is not what is required for, by definition, the horse cannot have the desire to go forward faster, and there is no more forward speed for the rider to contain.

Balance and rhythm

These two vital factors go hand in hand, as you cannot have one without the other.

To balance the horse keep his head up and use enough leg every stride to encourage the horse's hind legs to come further underneath him and support his weight. Thus the shoulders become lighter and can come off the ground more freely with every stride. The horse is then in a good attitude and balance to jump the fence, and will find it easy to do so. If the rider lets the horse put his head down, he will put more weight on to his forehand, the hind legs will not come so far under his body and he will find it difficult to jump, at best producing a flat jump (see Chapter 9).

The aim is to balance the horse so that he has rhythm and keeps an even tempo and length of stride, just as you would if approaching a jump on your own feet. Some horses find this is difficult and it requires practice and training to maintain balance and rhythm all the way to the fence.

Wait for the fence to come to you

Having got the horse going forward with impulsion, in balance, and therefore going with rhythm, jumping is easy if you can also remember the final golden rule. The rider must wait for the fence to come to him and not to be anxious either to see a stride (judge the take-off point) or to get to the fence. Instead of thinking, 'Where is it?', the rider should think, 'Keep coming, keep coming.' If you have the confidence to keep coming to a fence, going forward with the horse's head up so that he is balanced, and just wait for the fence to come to you, you will never have to worry about 'seeing a stride'.

I was taught to look for a stride, to judge where to take off, by saying, 'One, two, three, jump', or 'Kick, kick, kick, jump'. This is asking for trouble because when looking for a stride the rider says to himself, 'Where is it, where is it?', instinctively keeping the hand brake on while looking for his stride, and at the same time using no accelerator (the legs). The horse's head comes up, his back hollows and the hind legs trail out behind him, then the rider suddenly sees his stride, lets go the reins and kicks. The horse's head goes down, balance is lost on to the forehand, the outline gets longer and any remaining impulsion is lost – all of this, just in front of the fence when the horse is about to take off. The result is usually a long flat jump or the horse has to put in a very short extra stride in order to rebalance himself before taking off.

To practise the golden rules, keep the legs on the horse all the time and use them as necessary to keep the horse going forward and maintain his impulsion, and his balance with his shoulder coming freely off the ground. Keep contact with the reins to stop him speeding up and to help him remain in balance. If it is then necessary for him to shorten or lengthen his strides, he should have the impulsion to do so. The length of the strides can be altered progressively and evenly over three or four strides; this reduces the risk of losing balance. These three rules apply to all jumping, whether cross-country and racing or in the show jumping arena.

83 The horse in a good balance and going forward with impulsion on the approach to the fence, although the rider is a little behind the movement. Ideally the canter stride could be rounder

THE STYLE

When jumping always use the forward seat as the rider is already in the correct position, balanced and ready for take-off (see Chapter 5 The Position). He should have his weight off his seat bones and going down through his knees on to the balls of his feet, even if or when his seat bones are touching the saddle. The reason for this is that if the rider's weight is back on his seat bones, in an effort not to get left behind he will have to throw his weight forward in anticipation of the moment of take-off. Inevitably he will then get in front of the movement of the horse and have to support himself with his hands on the horse's neck and grip with his calves. Getting in front of the movement of the horse and out of balance makes it more difficult for the horse

to jump the fence. If the weight is off the seat bones as the horse takes off, his shoulders and neck come up and all the rider has to do is to remain standing on the balls of his feet and collapse at the hips to let his chest tip forward to meet the withers. The rider, therefore, absorbs the upward and forward movement of the take-off by flexing at the hips and leaning forward.

The line from the elbow to the bit should remain straight, that is through the forearm and hand and down the rein. The aim is to keep a constant contact, and for the hand to follow the horse's head forward and down, but to be able to do this takes balance, practice and feel. As it can hurt the horse and damage his confidence if the rider does not follow the movement of the horse's head and neck, or gets left behind, or even jabs him in the mouth,

84–90 A series showing how to jump a grid. In the first the rein contact is good, allowing the horse to drop his head and neck to look at the cross pole. The rider is in a good balance, still in the forward seat with the weight on the knee and the ball of the foot. In the second he has collapsed his hips, allowing his chest to dip toward the withers to go forward as the horse takes off. In the third he is beginning to sit up as the horse lands so the weight comes behind the lower leg. He is not interfering with the reins and has the correct straight line from the elbow to the bit. In the fourth he comes forward again, still in a good balance and with a loose rein, allowing the horse to use himself through the grid. In the fifth he has come back into the saddle on landing, but with his weight on the knees and the balls of the feet he is able to come forward again to keep in balance with the horse in the sixth. He is just starting to sit up for landing in the seventh

84

87

88

it is better for beginners to give too much with the reins. Nothing stops a horse or pony quicker than having continually to support the rider over the fence with his mouth, or being jabbed in the mouth.

After take-off, as the horse nears the apex of his jump, the rider should have his weight still in the stirrup irons on the balls of his feet, be gripping with his knees, bent at the hips and reaching forward with his hands to allow the horse to stretch and use his head and neck.

As the horse starts to come down the rider begins to sit up, bringing his upper body back, and allows his lower legs to move forward to wherever is necessary to support him on landing. As the horse lands the reins must support the horse so he can regain his balance and move straight away from the fence. The rider has to bring his balance forward

again as he lands so that he is in the forward seat for the move-off.

THE FAULTS

One of the most common and serious problems for beginners is getting left behind over a fence (see photograph 91). If the horse is jabbed in the mouth his head will come up, his back will hollow and it will be painful and difficult for him to clear the fence. The most common reasons for getting left behind are that the rider's reins are too long and that his weight is too far back on the seat bones. If a rider does find himself left behind, the vital factor is quickly to open the fingers so that the reins can slip through; this will at least avoid jabbing the horse in the mouth and destroying his confidence.

85

86

89

90

The other extreme of getting in front of the horse is less damaging but does lead to a loss of balance. If the rider's weight is over the shoulders on take-off, the excess weight will make it difficult for the horse to bring his shoulders up and he will tend to jump flat. However this is a fault on the right side for the beginner, and is a lot better than getting left behind, especially when the fences are only small.

It is very important not to get in front of the movement over the top of the fence, because on landing the only ways in which the rider can stop himself tipping over the horse's front are by using his hands on the neck to support himself and by gripping with his calves (see photograph 92).

If, for whatever reason, the calves are used for gripping, the lower legs will swing back and the heels and knees come up as the rider tenses in his effort to grip. Then, if anything goes wrong on landing, the lower leg will flip up and in this position the rider cannot support the horse as he lands. The rider will tend to fall on to the neck just when the horse needs help to bring his head up. Gripping with the lower leg rather than the knee is a major reason for falling off. When the lower leg flips back the rider tends to lose his balance and tumble off if the horse slips, pecks, jinks or stumbles on landing.

Another important aspect of the style over the fence is that the rider should not look down or drop his head because this tends to tip him forward; the lower leg will come up and balance will be lost, as already described. The rider must look ahead. If he looks down, sooner or later that is where he will end up – down on the ground where he is looking.

91 The author demonstrating getting left behind over the fence. He has opened his fingers to let the reins slip through so as not to interfere with the horse's mouth

92 The rider has fallen forward too much on landing, forcing her to balance on the horse's neck and unbalancing the horse

93 The rider leaning back much too much on landing. She has had to let the reins slip through her fingers

Suddenly dropping the reins before take-off tends to throw the horse off balance. It also makes the horse wonder if the rider really wants to jump the fence and puts him in control, so that if he wants to run out or to stop, he can do so. The contact can be gradually eased once the horse is committed to the fence, but one should never suddenly drop the contact, as too often the sudden loss of balance will cause all but the most generous horse to stop.

Another similar fault is for riders to fall forward during the last few strides, normally because they are either anxious to get to the fence or allow the horse to pull them forward, causing loss of balance to both parties. In either instance the rider must retain his balance, keep the horse's head up and maintain contact all the way to the fence.

THE STAGES OF LEARNING

When starting to jump it is important for the rider to progress gradually and until he is sure of staying in balance it is better to lean further forward and avoid jabbing the horse in the mouth than get left behind. The beginner should concentrate on getting the horse to go forward and to establish the best possible balance. As he reaches the first pole, whether it is a trotting or placing pole or a tiny fence, he can allow with the reins until there is no contact with the mouth and concentrate on staying in balance with the horse. This is easier if the horse is experienced, and the obstacles are very small.

Start by trotting over a pole on the ground, then a cavalletti, then a pole on the ground 9 ft in front of a small cross bar. Progress to jumping out of the canter by moving the pole to 6 yds before the fence, so the horse comes over the pole and takes one stride, then try at 10 yds (two strides) and, if this goes smoothly and the rider stays in balance, progress to a pole on the ground 14 yds (three strides for horses) before a cross bar. The fence can be changed into a single bar or a small parallel, still keeping the placing pole 14 yds in front of it.

This exercise with three canter strides before the fence helps the rider to develop an idea of maintaining the rhythm, waiting for the fence to come to him and not rushing the horse into the fence. Alternatively use a trotting pole 9 ft before a cross pole which is no higher than 3 ft, and then put poles in multiples of 4 yds apart before the trotting pole. Grids are also a great help in developing a rider's sense of balance; as the poles on the ground help the horse to remain in balance and at a good position for take-off, all the rider has to think about is staying in balance with the horse.

Further distances for grids are specified in the next chapter (page 74). It is important to remember that the distances mentioned are for the average striding horse. They must be built to suit the individual horse or pony so, for example, they should be reduced for shorter striding horses and ponies.

When the rider is confident that he can stay with the horse, then he can start to maintain rein contact throughout the grid. It is important he does not do this too early, when he is still relying on heels and hands to hang on. If he is not in balance, he cannot keep a consistent contact, and will interfere with the horse's vital freedom to stretch his head and neck forward and down in mid-air over a fence.

When the rider's position is established in grid work then he can try single fences. With these he must think about the three principles, keeping the horse going forward, remaining in balance and waiting for the fence to come to him. It is difficult to do if he still needs to think about how to keep in the correct position before, during and after the fence. Therefore it is important for the rider to be able to stay in balance with the horse in grids, without

94 Although the balance is a little behind the leg, it is a pretty good position for a child jumping at speed. There is a nice soft rein contact with the pony's mouth

having to think how to do it, before he tackles single fences.

The first single fences the rider tries should be small uprights and then he can progress to small spreads. The approach into all types of fences is similar but spreads may need a little more pace and a little more impulsion. With a triple bar it is important to take off close to the front bar because it is a wide spread, and the further the take-off from it the more difficult it is to clear the back bar.

When approaching a fence the rider must be committed to jumping it. As soon as he is not determined to jump it, this seems to bring his legs away from the horse's sides and the message goes down the reins to the horse. He has an uncanny way of knowing if the rider is truly committed to jumping, and if the rider is not determined and positive in his approach all but the most generous horses will lose confidence and stop.

Learning to jump is great fun as long as the rider is not overfaced or frightened. If he is, then it becomes difficult to commit himself to going over the fence. Take care, therefore, to progress gradually, and only try a more difficult fence after the easier one has been mastered. If there is a problem, revert to an earlier and simpler obstacle. Practise as much as possible but do not make the horse bored by always jumping the same obstacles; vary the exercises, and never jump him so much that he becomes tired and fed up.

9 · TRAINING THE HORSE AND PONY

Schooling develops greater control over the horse. There are many different methods of schooling and I have followed the principle that if a method works with a horse, if he understands what is needed, then that is likely to be the correct formula for that horse. Provided the rider understands what he is doing, provided the way he is achieving it is successful, then it is an acceptable method. People are different, as are horses, so there are many methods of achieving a desired result. All I can do is explain my aims when schooling and then the exercises I use to develop them.

FORWARDNESS

The first aim is for a horse to have the desire to go freely forward in a relaxed manner, in response to the leg aids, but at this first stage only on a loose rein (see photograph 95). He has to learn to trot willingly forward without having to be constantly kicked, and to keep going forward from a gentle leg aid. To develop this responsiveness to the leg aids, start with nudges or taps of the leg and if he does not respond, encourage him to do so in future by using stronger aids, kicking him harder or reinforcing the leg aids with the voice and, if necessary, a schooling whip.

Most young horses tend to be reluctant to go forward and are best worked in an area where there is enough room to get up some momentum, but not so much that they can gather speed and run away. There will be some that are tense and dash off and these need calming down, in which case a smaller enclosed arena is a better working area. Select a schooling place which suits the temperament of your horse and make use of situations which might help him to go forward, such as following another horse or heading for home.

CONTACT

The second aim can only be achieved once the horse wants to go forward and is responding to the leg aids; then the rider can start to work towards establishing a consistent contact with the mouth through the reins (see photograph 96). At this stage it does not matter about the position of the horse's head as long as he wants to go forward and accept the rein contact. The aim is for the rider to be able to feel in his hands a contact with the mouth which is soft (not pulling), elastic (not leaning) and con-

95 A horse going forward on a loose rein

Friends together

Jumping in a pair

Going for a canter

96 A horse going forward to a contact, but at this early stage he is still on his forehand

97 A horse in a good outline and taking a good contact at the working trot

98 The rider has opened his fingers and leaned forward to allow the horse to stretch forward and down, and the horse is doing so without falling onto his forehand

sistent (not intermittent). Whatever the head does the pressure of the rider's hands remains the same, therefore the hands must follow the movement of the head wherever it goes so that the horse starts to realize that he cannot escape the contact.

When the horse begins to accept the contact the rider should then aim to encourage the horse to want to take the contact forward and down and to establish the soft rounded novice outline shown in photograph 97. When the horse is drawing the contact forward and down correctly the rider can soften his fingers. If he opens his fingers the horse should stretch his neck as in photograph 98. If the horse raises his head as in photograph 99, then the bit should be moved in his mouth and the legs kept positively on his sides. If he tries to drop the contact and bring his head towards his chest then maintain the contact and ride forward to the bit.

Although the horse should always go forward it must be at the speed the rider wants him to go. The horse must not be pulling and it must be possible for the rider to use his legs without the horse pulling harder or running off. In this way the speed of the horse is governed by the legs rather than the reins. The horse is then 'waiting for the rider'.

If the horse is going too fast, the natural tendency is for the rider to pull on the reins, but the horse

99 A horse raising his head, hollowing his back and not taking a true contact

will only shorten his neck and hollow his back, all of which will restrict his ability to use himself in his paces. Every time the rider feels the horse is even thinking about speeding up he must use the half halt. To do this he applies the aids for the downward transition, maintaining the contact and containing with the hands, but without pulling back, and with the seat and legs pushes the horse up to this contact. The effect of this is to steady the horse, because more pressure is being brought to bear on the mouth from the increased leg aid, but just before he changes down into the next pace the rider relaxes and allows with the hands so that the horse can go forward again. This is known as the half halt because the aids for a full halt are relaxed halfway through and the halt is not completed.

The half halt is a difficult movement for the rider to master and the untrained horse to learn with a beginner. When training the horse it is important to be satisfied with a comparatively small response to the half halt, as long as it is the result of using the legs and seat and not of pulling back with the hands; the half halt is not simply a hook with the hand on one of the reins. In the early stages it might take a whole series of half halts over a considerable distance to achieve the same results that a more experienced horse and rider would produce in one stride.

The free-going horse will need more half halts than a lazy one. Keep applying them, preferably on a circle if the horse is pulling or wanting to go faster, until it is possible to use the legs and ride him forward every stride.

The rider controls the forwardness of the horse through the half halt and not by pulling on the reins.

STRAIGHTNESS

The third aim is straightness. The horse's hind legs should step along the same tracks as the corresponding forelegs, whether on a straight line or on a bend. If they step to one side he is crooked. The problem is that all horses are naturally crooked and training is needed to correct this.

100 A horse moving straight with the hindlegs following in the tracks of their corresponding foreleg

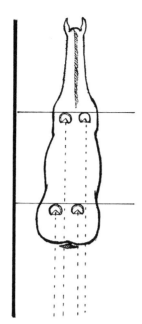

A horse which is not straight

The first stage is to try to bend the horse slightly to the inside on a circle so that he is not looking to the outside or going around like a board. The rider aims to stop him leaning on either the rider's inside or outside leg and at first this is normally easier to achieve in the walk.

When the rider applies his leg on the girth the horse should walk around it rather than lean on it. To achieve this the inside leg is applied by the girth and the horse is ridden into a circle. It is a good idea to use an object such as a fence or an oil drum to turn around as this helps stop the horse falling in. The rider has to adjust his hands to keep that soft contact and to point the horse's head in the direction required so there is no more bend in the neck than the rest of the body. The legs are used to keep the horse going forward and to control the shoulders and the hindquarters, which should follow the head and not fall out or in. The seat is used to keep the horse going forward and to help the rider stay in balance.

BALANCE

The horse should now be going forward relatively straight into a contact. In order for that contact to be consistent the horse needs to be balanced. If he loses his balance, usually it results in his leaning on the contact, which will make him take shorter and often quicker strides.

To establish balance the first aim is rhythm. The speed of this rhythm should be such that in all the paces the horse should not be going so slowly that the work is laboured nor so fast that it is hurried. The rider must find a speed to the rhythm which suits the horse and in which he is most relaxed and comfortable and therefore best able to find his balance. This will vary from horse to horse.

The most common way for a horse to lose his balance is forward and downwards. The tendency is to lean on the contact and put his weight on to the shoulder, neck and head. This leaning on the contact is very different from taking the contact down and away (see photograph 98), for then no additional weight falls on the shoulders which are still light and free to move easily. The rider must distinguish between a horse who takes the contact down and out and one who takes it down to lean on, as the latter is losing his balance (see photograph 101). Consequently he will be likely to lose his rhythm, quicken and/or shorten his strides.

101 A horse taking the contact down to lean on the bit, rather than taking the contact down and out

The way to change this misdirection of the balance is to engage the hindquarters (see photograph 102), which helps bring up the shoulders and head. This is achieved through the half halt and as each one ends by lightening the rein contact it will also encourage the horse to carry himself.

102 A horse in a good balance with hinds engaged and taking a good contact with the bit

about making the horse supple so that he becomes loose and relaxed, easier to flex and bend in both directions, and less likely to resist and stiffen those vital muscles in the neck and back.

The exercises

I do most of my work on a circle. The major exception is in the early stages when teaching a lazy horse to go forwards; then long straight lines are best. After the desire to go forward has been developed it is easier to train on a circle because it helps reduce resistance. The horse is softer in the hand and more relaxed in his back when the rider asks for a slight bend. On a straight line the horse finds it easier to stiffen against the rider.

With lazy horses I use big circles as it is easier to keep them going forward, and until they are going forward you cannot train them further. With tense, energetic horses I reduce the size as this helps to stop them wanting to go faster all the time, and helps calm them down.

It is easier to keep a horse balanced if the circles are round, as then the turns will be smooth. If they are a poor shape, there will be sharp turns and flatter sections and this makes it more difficult to keep the rhythm. To make a circle round think of

The contact will only be consistent when the horse is balanced. Without that contact it is difficult for the horse to keep his balance and move with regular paces, because there is nothing for the rider to ride to with the legs and seat. This is why it is so important for a rider to develop a sense of balance so that his weight is not shifted in the saddle and he is able to keep his hands still to establish a consistent contact. Riders who move their hands, thus preventing a consistent contact, may wonder why every time they try a transition the horse puts his head in the air, or why when they ask for lengthened strides the horse runs. By moving the hands they are often shaking the horse off the contact; he has nothing to take hold of to help keep himself balanced and they have nothing to which they can ride forward.

SUPPLENESS

While working on establishing forwardness, contact, straightness and balance it is also important to think

103 Cantering the young horse. The forward seat takes the weight off the horse's back to give the back muscles more freedom to operate and encourage them to stretch

it as having four points – north, south, east and west: on reaching one point the rider looks for the next.

It can help to keep the horse balanced if the turns are thought of as a series of almost straight steps. It is a common fault to pull the horse around the circle with the inside rein; the bend then becomes excessive and a shoulder falls out. The horse can only keep his balance if there is no more bend in his neck than there is in his body.

Variations on the circle, such as figures of eight and serpentines, are useful exercises to keep a horse soft and supple and to help develop his balance. The changes in direction also help to stop him leaning on one side of the bit.

Transitions are a key exercise. They help to establish greater control over the horse and to make him more supple. He has to maintain his balance and the rein contact throughout the transition, so he should neither throw up his head nor lean on the bit. Everything discussed earlier about getting a horse to take a contact applies during transitions. If he puts his head up in a transition, the bit has to be moved in his mouth and the legs kept positively on his sides; if he drops the bit in the transition, the contact must be maintained whilst riding him firmly forward.

LATERAL WORK

An important stage in the horse's training is when he starts lateral work (goes sideways at the same time as forwards). I usually start teaching a horse to go sideways when out hacking. When going down a track in walk or trot the horse can learn to move away from the leg without getting anxious and tense. In the more natural surroundings I find horses tend to be less resistant.

Going sideways is not just a dressage movement, it is generally useful, for instance, in opening and shutting gates. To teach a horse to go sideways it is best to start in walk. Throughout the movement the rider keeps his weight on both seat bones and takes care not to lose his balance. The horse is kept almost straight but with a slight flexion away from the direction towards which he is being asked to move. The leg is applied just behind the girth with a tap, tap, tap. It can be reinforced by taps with a schooling whip and this is one occasion when spurs can be useful. It is a mistake to keep thumping at

104 A horse being taught to go sideways in a leg yield to the left

the horse with the leg as this is disconcerting for him and will only make him tense as well as unbalance the rider. The horse should move forwards and sideways from one side of the track to the other. Alternatively he can be turned towards a fence and the aids can be applied, keeping him at an angle of about 30 degrees to the fence, with a slight bend in the opposite direction to that in which he is moving. As he masters this he can be turned away from the fence and again kept at an angle of about 30 degrees to it while moving forwards and sideways.

With all lateral work it is again important that the hands do not pull back and stop the horse going forward while endeavouring to send him sideways.

LUNGEING

Lungeing is an important aspect of training. The special advantage is that with the trainer on the ground the horse does not have to worry about a weight on his back. It is a way of teaching a young horse the first lessons in obedience. It gives a horse the chance to find out about new experiences (for example, wearing a bridle and saddle, going into a contact), without the rider providing additional disturbances. It is also a means of helping a horse to establish his balance and rhythm so that all three paces are neither laboured nor rushed.

Some special equipment is needed for lungeing (see photograph 105). It is best to use a lunge cavesson but, if one is not available, either the lunge rein can be run through the inside ring of the bit, up over the poll and down to be attached to the outside ring of the bit, or a tight-fitting headcollar can be used. It is not advisable to attach the rein to the bit of a young horse who has not learnt to accept a contact; either a headcollar or cavesson should be used.

The lunge cavesson or headcollar must be fastened tight enough to prevent its slipping round. It is usually put over a bridle, as in photograph 105. The lunge rein is attached to the front ring of the cavesson and it is this rein which is the trainer's main means of control. The aim is to keep a constant, even contact with the horse through the rein in the same way as when riding. The rein is held in the left hand when the horse is on the left rein and vice versa. The free rein is looped and held in the right hand together with the whip (see photograph 106). If a saddle is worn, the stirrups should be run up or taken off so that they will not hang down and bang the horse.

It is best to lunge in an enclosed area to help keep the horse's concentration, and if necessary, this can be constructed in a field using the hedges on two sides and straw bales or poles between jump uprights, buckets or barrels on the others.

105 A horse equipped for lungeing

106 Starting the horse off on the lunge, keeping level with his back legs and maintaining a taut contact in the lunge rein

107 Lungeing correctly with a taut lunge line

To start a horse on the lunge the trainer has to do a good deal of walking. With the horse standing still the trainer walks back until level with his hind legs so that the whip can be pointed behind the legs (see photograph 106). The horse is then asked to walk on and if he does not respond, the voice is used more emphatically and he is tapped with the whip just above the hocks or on the hindquarters. If he walks on, but then tries to stop, the trainer should keep close to the back legs so that the horse goes around him and cannot stop and look at him. As the horse begins to understand that he must move around the trainer then the rein is gradually fed out so that he goes on a larger and larger circle, but with the trainer still remaining level with the hind legs. As the horse becomes more responsive to the voice, whip and hand the trainer need not walk so much and eventually he can stand on one point, level with the horse's shoulder, with the horse working on a true circle (see photograph 107).

To teach the horse to stop, first the trainer talks to him saying, 'woahh' or 'waalk'; second, he tugs

gently on the lunge rein; third, he changes his angle with the horse by moving towards his front end. If the horse still does not respond, then the trainer has to move and direct the horse towards a wall or fence. When he stops the trainer should not let him come in towards him, but should go out to him and reward him with the voice and a pat.

The whip acts as the rider's legs and is a very important part of lungeing. If the horse is rushing around, the trainer can keep the whip behind his back, but once the horse is settled, the whip can be pointed at the horse's hindquarters to encourage forward momentum as and when it is required. The lunge line should be kept taut at all times. If the horse starts to fall in and the lunge rein slackens, the whip can be pointed towards his head or shoulder, and if necessary waggled or flicked a little to keep the horse on a true circle.

The other important aid in lungeing is the voice. This is used in a high sharp tone to make the horse go forward and in a low tone to make him slow down. Its effect can be reinforced if used in conjunction with the whip (to go forward) or with the rein (to slow down).

The first lessons on the lunge for an untrained horse should be at the walk; trotting should only be started as his understanding, obedience and relaxation develop.

He can be lunged without side reins for a few sessions, but I use them from an early stage. I attach them at the top of the saddle, which means they are in a similar position to the rider's hands. In the beginning they should be so loose that they have no effect, but as the horse becomes relaxed and goes freely forward, they can be tightened progressively until the horse is not just going forward, but going forward into a contact (see photograph 108). At first he might not want to go forward into this contact and will have to be encouraged to do so (without making him tense) through the use of the voice and whip. Take care the side reins are never so tight that his head is pulled behind the vertical.

When the horse is being led to the lungeing area, and after he has finished, the side reins should be taken off the bit and hooked back on to the saddle to give the horse a free head carriage. If they are left on, the horse all too easily starts to fiddle in his mouth, avoiding taking a contact with the bit, as he is not being pushed forward.

108 A horse correctly taking the contact on the side reins forward and down

JUMPING

Introduce the horse to fences in as simple and quiet a manner as possible. This can be done on the lunge (without side reins) or with the rider. Lungeing is a good introduction as long as the horse is obedient on the lunge and the trainer is skilled at this activity. Novice riders who are trying to teach a horse to jump may be best advised to do so from the saddle.

Start training over trotting poles (4 ft 6 ins apart). Begin with one and build up to three, four and then five, so that the horse gets used to trotting over them in a rhythm, going forward and straight. Progress to trotting over the poles followed by a low cross bar fence 9 ft away (see photographs 109 and 110). This can be done by taking away the fourth trotting pole and making the cross bar at the fifth trotting pole. This is the simplest of all grids.

If this early training is being done from the saddle, the poles, and then the fence, can be in a straight line, but if the horse is being lunged, the trotting poles should be on a curve (see diagram) and the 4 ft 6 ins distance between them should be measured on the inside. When the cross bar is added for lungeing use wings as shown in the diagram.

If the horse is being lunged and does this exercise quietly, then start riding him, beginning with trotting poles, and repeating the exercises before adding another small fence 18 ft away. This is one canter

109–110 The first lessons in jumping, trotting poles to a small cross bar. Note how the rider has fallen too far forward over the cross pole

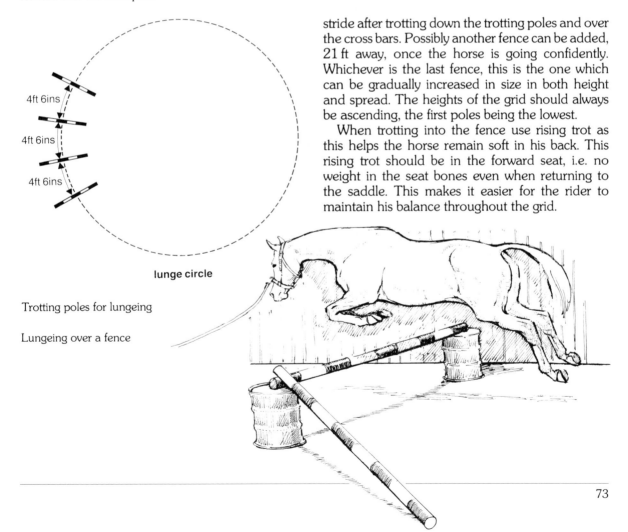

4ft 6ins

4ft 6ins

4ft 6ins

lunge circle

Trotting poles for lungeing

Lungeing over a fence

stride after trotting down the trotting poles and over the cross bars. Possibly another fence can be added, 21 ft away, once the horse is going confidently. Whichever is the last fence, this is the one which can be gradually increased in size in both height and spread. The heights of the grid should always be ascending, the first poles being the lowest.

When trotting into the fence use rising trot as this helps the horse remain soft in his back. This rising trot should be in the forward seat, i.e. no weight in the seat bones even when returning to the saddle. This makes it easier for the rider to maintain his balance throughout the grid.

If these exercises go well and the horse is confident and relaxed, progress to single fences, first uprights and then spreads. Start at the trot then go on to the canter. Return frequently to grid work, extending the number of fences and varying them to include different fences, bounces and shorter distances. When the horse works well through a variety of grids, first doubles, then combinations, can be introduced, and finally small courses. This is all done over a period of months, each new stage being progressed to only when the horse masters the easier one.

Grids, doubles and combinations must be built to suit the novice horse to give him confidence. The distances should be correct for him so that he is not frightened either by having to reach for a fence or taking off so close he crashes through it. Average stridings are 4 yds per horse's stride plus 2 yds for take-off, and 2 yds for landing, but for novice horses over small jumps distances may be slightly shorter. The vital consideration is that they should always be built to suit the horse so that he finds them easy.

The correct distances for the average horse are shown below, but they will need to be adjusted as circumstances dictate. For ponies, for short-striding horses and if the going is deep or uphill, the distances must be reduced; for long-striding horses or if the going is downhill, they must be extended.

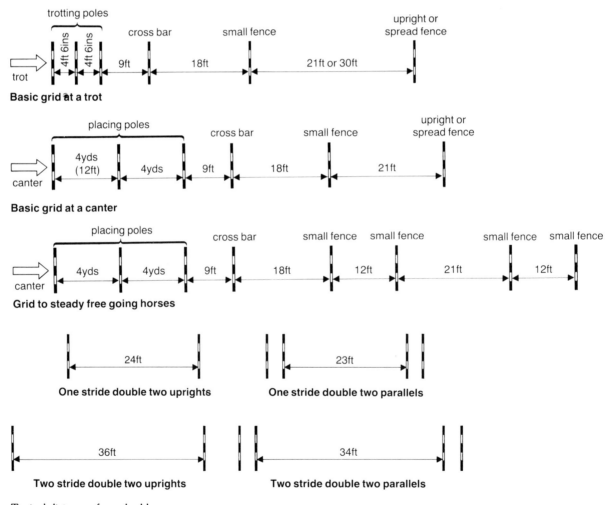

Typical distances for a double

The distances of grids can be varied as the horse progresses to help make him more athletic. In the first place the distances should be such that he neither has to shorten nor lengthen; later they can be shortened but by no more than 6 ins at a time, and only between the obstacles, not between placing or trotting poles. With closer distances the horse will learn to shorten his stride, to take off close to

111–114 Asking a horse to take off very close, 'putting him in deep'. Note the light contact at take off and the freedom being given to the horse over the fence. The horse has had to really use himself to clear the fence, making it difficult for the author to stay in balance. He does finally lose his balance on landing but with minimum ill effects as he opened his fingers over the fence to allow the horse to take as much rein as he needed

111

112

113

114

the fence and use himself to clear it. He will have to become sharper, more careful with his front legs and more supple in his body if he is to clear the fences. All this must be achieved without interference from the rider.

The aim in these jumping lessons should be to start with very easy work and progress gradually, building up on each stage. Little by little the fences can be made more demanding, but only as the horse has mastered the previous exercise. He must have been able to jump them in good, confident style before trying anything more difficult. On the approach he should go forward to the obstacle with balance and rhythm. At the obstacle he should drop his head to look at the fence, which should free his shoulders to come off the ground, then he can bend his back and round his body over the fence. At this stage a relaxed forward-going approach is more important than a spectacular jump. If a problem arises, go back to an easier stage and build up again.

The other important aspect of jumping lessons is to try to stop before the horse has to make such an effort that he frightens himself and starts to lose confidence. If he does have to struggle to get over a fence, put the fence down, make the distance as easy as possible and finish over something which is not difficult. Reward him when he has done well.

If a horse is not jumping well and not going to a fence in a good style, it is essential to discover the reason. It could be that the rider is nervous, the fence too big, the horse has lost his confidence or is simply being obstinate. If the cause can be found, then commonsense is usually all that is needed to find the remedy – e.g. lower fences for nervous riders and horses, firm handling for obstinate horses. Remember, a horse cannot be forced to jump. He must be kept over small fences until he really enjoys it and wants to go to his fences.

CROSS-COUNTRY JUMPING

I find there is very little difference between my preparation for show jumping and for cross-country. I do very little special schooling with the cross-country horse other than to familiarize him with ditches, water, banks and drops. Show and cross-country fences are approached in the same way in terms of the golden rules – going forward with balance and rhythm, and waiting for the fence to come to you. Speed is the only difference. The golden rules are usually easier to achieve across country because the horse is galloping and so is more likely to be going forward. This speed, however, will change according to the type of fence. Some fences cannot be jumped fast; these include drops, coffins and fences into water.

Much of the familiarization for cross-country can be done when hacking. Puddles and streams can be paddled through, the gutters on the roadside jumped, banks hopped on to and over, and small ditches popped over. It is important for the horse to be confident about ditches, since then they can be ridden like any other fence.

COMMON PROBLEMS

For all training the rider needs to plan a programme so that lessons do not last too long and the same thing is not repeated so often that the horse becomes bored and his muscles tired. There should be plenty of variety and nothing difficult should be tackled until the easier lesson has been learnt. The endless problems must be approached logically. If a horse is not doing what is required, the rider must question whether his mount understands what he is supposed to be doing, if he is physically capable of doing what is asked, or whether he is frightened. It is quite rare that a horse is simply being stubborn. Whatever the problem the rider should stop, stand back from the situation and consider the possible reasons.

The following are some of the most common problems horse and rider encounter, the possible reasons for them and possible solutions. The important point when there is a problem is to identify the cause, for most problems require different remedies.

Problem: horse lacking forwardness

CAUSE	POSSIBLE REMEDY
Does not understand.	Read chapter 6 on the aids.
Idle.	Use stronger leg and schooling whip or spurs.
Bored.	Give him a holiday, vary work.
Tired.	Give more fittening work, if immature, give shorter lessons.
Frightened.	Check bit is not too strong. Check for other physical problems (teeth, back, etc).
Obstinate.	Tackle problem from different angle. Try going towards home, or behind another horse.

Problem: running/strides too fast

Does not understand.	Read chapter 6 on the aids.
Loss of balance.	Use half halt to balance and engage hindquarters.
Running towards pain.	Examine mouth, check for sores, cuts, rough teeth. Noseband may pinch. Bit may be too severe.
Worried/tense.	Reassurance from voice, supportive, quiet but firm leg and hand. Clear aids but not severe.
Running towards home.	Work on diagonals, but not directly towards home.
Hurried in past/pushed out of natural rhythm.	Use half halt. Do not allow him to continue to hurry.

Problem: rider losing balance and bumping in saddle

Tension in head/arms/hands tummy/back, gripping with calves, pushing down with heels, weight on balls of feet.	Try to isolate problem and relax. Let the movement happen and follow it. Do not lean forward, keep seat bones in the saddle.
Sitting crooked.	Keep even weight on both seat bones, sit upright, do not let foot rise off stirrup or the heel ride up the side of the horse.

Problem: horse losing balance

Loss of rhythm.	Use half halt.
Leaning on bit.	Push up with legs and seat to engage quarters. Half halt.
Not straight.	Use appropriate leg aids and more schooling.
Lack of support from rider.	Use more leg, seat and hand as supportive aids.
Rider not balanced.	See above.
Rider asking too much.	Revert to easier lessons.

10 · EVENTS

Some people ride solely for the fun of being on horseback and hacking across country. An increasing number, however, like to ride for a purpose, to hunt and compete. This chapter gives some idea of what is involved and the preparations which are necessary. Events exist for all levels and a horse or pony who has received the basic training discussed in the previous chapter should be capable of taking part in the easiest grades.

THE PONY CLUB AND RIDING CLUBS

Most riders start by joining the Pony Club or a riding club. Both organize rallies and clinics for instruction, and competitions of a basic standard. They provide a stepping stone on to the lower rungs of the ladder for the ambitious competitor and a great opportunity to meet people who share similar interests and with whom riding can be enjoyed.

I owe much to the Pony Club. I started with the Ledbury then moved to join the Beaufort. I made many friends and we were so naughty I must have been a misery to the teachers – until I was told I had to do my first dressage test as a candidate for the team. Although the first test was a joke, the fact that I had been considered for the team made me take matters more seriously. I was thirteen years old when I first went on the lunge and I found it agony, but I knew I had to do it if I wanted to have a chance of being selected. We had, too, the inspiration of such good instructors as the ex-Olympic riders Colonel Frank Weldon and Colonel Alec Scott.

The Pony Club got me going, as I had to work very hard to make the grade. The first year I was chosen for the team I was eliminated, but the second year we won the Area Trial. I learnt so much

with the Pony Club that when I graduated to adult events the transition into novice horse trials was an easy one. It was only when I progressed to advanced level that I discovered how much more I still had to learn.

When I was a member the main event was the Pony Club Horse Trials Championships, but today there are opportunities in all spheres – show jumping, dressage, polo and the Prince Philip Mounted Games.

A riding club is the adult version of the Pony Club, although children may also join. One of the best aspects of these clubs is that members can join in at a very basic level and go to such easy events as rallies. For most of these all that is needed is a semi-fit horse or pony, a hard hat, jodhpurs with sensible shoes or boots, or breeches and boots (see photograph 115).

HUNTING

Hunting is another activity which helped to make my riding. It is the difference between children of today and my generation that we did have a chance to do some fantastic hunting. I remember one day, when hunting on a 14.2hh pony, when we had a four-, five- and six-mile points all in the same day. Such days as this helped teach us to cross the country, to pick a route, choose sensible fences and to look after our ponies, otherwise they would be too tired to get to the end of the day. This type of hunting helps the rider to develop a natural affinity with the horse as well as feel and balance. Having to face the unexpected teaches one to improvise, to be able to get out of trouble, and this is what makes a great rider.

115 A rider suitably equipped for a Pony Club rally

Hunting takes more preparation than Pony Club and riding club rallies. The horse or pony has to be controllable but fit, having had regular exercise on the roads or, even better, trotting up hills. The rider needs to be turned out smartly, with hard hat, jacket, stock or tie, jodhpurs or breeches and boots, crop and gloves.

Etiquette is important for this traditional sport. The Master should be greeted, 'Good morning, Master', and the cap or field money paid to the secretary. Care should be taken to keep the horse's or pony's heels away from hounds. When the hunt moves off remember to keep behind the Field Master, shut gates, keep off fields sown with young grass or grain and not to run into the backside of another horse because he may kick. Any horse who tends to kick should wear a red ribbon around his tail.

SHOW JUMPING

Before going show jumping, horse and rider need plenty of training at home and practice over courses, although today there are opportunities to start in the arena over very low courses. Clear round jumping for children and adults, which may have fences as low as 2ft, is a popular feature at many shows.

Walking the course is a very important aspect of show jumping. The first fence must be looked at and plans made as to how to get to it. Ideally, if the beginning of the course is on the right hand, then the rider should start on the right lead. The aim is to select a route between the fences which makes it easier to keep the horse going forwards with impulsion, balance and rhythm, and this needs careful planning. Pulling the horse sharply around

116 Riders set for a day's hunting

a corner should always be avoided as this results in loss of balance and rhythm.

Doubles and combinations are some of the trickiest fences and their distances must be walked. A distance of 24 ft between the two fences in a double is an easy single non-jumping stride for most horses, but will be long for a pony and could be short for a big horse. In principle if the distance is short for the horse or pony, approach slowly, but fast enough to jump the first element; if it is long, then speed up. However, as your ability improves, a more sophisticated approach can be used and this will be covered in my next book.

The space in the ring should be used. It is unnecessarily difficult to turn into a fence with only three or four strides before it when seven or eight are possible. It is also more of a risk to approach the fence at an angle (except in a timed jump-off) than to be absolutely straight at it.

Consider the going. If it is slippery, studs in the shoes help, and corners have to be ridden very carefully to keep the horse balanced.

At the end of walking the course I always look away and picture in my mind each of the fences in the order they are to be jumped. Then I look back and check that my memory was correct. I also keep in my mind how I plan to ride each fence, the rhythm with which I will approach, the speed for each fence and the exact route and turns I am going to follow.

The warming-up will depend on the horse and rider. When starting to jump at a show it helps the horse if a similar routine is used to that when jumping at home, i.e. the same type of flat work, then trotting poles, followed by a placing pole to a cross bar, according to what has been found best for the horse. The important factors are that both horse and rider are alert, relaxed and jumping in

A Pony Club display

Cantering on the beach

Saving time by turning in the air

good style, with forward momentum and balance, but without rushing.

On entering the ring take care not to start before the bell. If you are not sure whether it has rung, wait and look towards the judges – they will always ring it again. The corners must be ridden carefully; if you go into them balanced and with forward momentum, then the horse should not have to be pulled around and unbalanced. Like a car, as long as he is well set up for the corner the horse can accelerate out of it, which makes it easier to jump the fence.

If a fence is hit, it is a mistake to look back, because this usually unbalances the horse and there is still the next fence to be jumped.

If the horse has to flatten over a fence to get out of trouble, it is important to balance him well before the following fence. If he has had to make a big effort, the rider must make the next fence as easy as possible for him because asking for another big effort could result in a loss of confidence and the horse might stop. It is vital to come to the next fence well balanced and with plenty of impulsion.

If the horse jumps a good round, do not forget to reward him with the voice and pats.

117 Show jumping events of varying standards are held all over Britain throughout the year

DRESSAGE

Dressage requires more discipline and preparation than other equestrian sports. If the work cannot be done well at home, it is rare that the excitement of competing will make it any better; usually it will be much worse. A dressage competition is a test of the training done at home.

It helps if you set out an arena at home so that horse and rider can get used to riding in a confined area. Eight tins or buckets to mark the four corners and the markers A, C, B and E are sufficient.

Learning the test can be done with a pencil and paper and then by walking around the carpet at home. Also I keep riding it through in my mind until I can remember it easily and without any reference to the test sheet. On the horse I practise the salute and particular movements, but not in the sequence of the test, as most horses will then start to anticipate the movements. I make sure I ride into the corners so that I can make better use of the space of the arena, but when I ride the test I am careful not to overdo this and run the risk of upsetting the balance and rhythm. It is more important to make the turns smoothly.

When schooling, try to develop accuracy by using selected landmarks such as docks, thistles or cowpats in the field at which to halt, trot, turn left. Accuracy earns many marks.

The riding-in at the show itself demands a special skill. Many people lose their dressage competition outside the arena. Riders tend to become tense, over-react and make the horse tense. It is important to remain relaxed and not to get upset if the horse makes mistakes. The horse needs to be prepared in a relaxed way so that he can be ridden freely forward in a good rhythm. It is best to minimize the practising of the movements and not to ask for any until he is relaxed and accepts the use of the leg. The horse will then be fresh and interested when he goes in the arena. I spend most of my time riding-in trying to make the horse calm and stretch his head forward and down (see photograph 118). Once he is in that state, riding the movements is easier. Then about ten minutes before the test I ask for a more positive contact and more impulsion, and practise a few of the movements.

It is important to allow enough time for a nervous horse to get rid of his excitement of being at a show. Lungeing can be useful as the horse can let go of

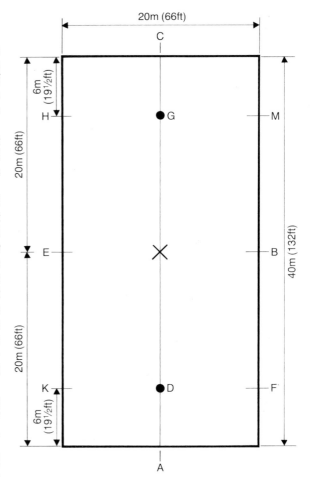

Plan of 20 x 40 arena

Plan of 20 × 40 dressage arena

his excess energy without upsetting himself or the rider. There is a great skill in riding the test so as not to throw away unnecessary marks. Even if the horse cannot do the movements, if the rider tries to make the work smooth, rhythmical and accurate it is surprising how many marks can be accumulated.

It is very important for the rider to sit up, look where he is going and be unruffled even when something goes wrong. Look as if everything is going according to plan: never allow the mind to linger on what has just happened. Always stay calm and think forward to the movements ahead.

The general impression helps. If the judge sees

118 The author riding-in for dressage in the forward seat

a well-turned out horse, whose rider has polished boots and smart clothes, he usually thinks of them in terms of higher marks than he would a scruffy child, with jacket undone, on an unplaited pony.

Finally, a friendly smile helps to keep the judge on the side of the competitor.

HORSE TRIALS

Horse trials combines the show jumping and dressage already discussed, together with the cross-country. It is a busy day and requires careful planning if everything is to be done as well as possible. It also requires a fit horse or pony. At least one month's regular work is needed for ponies, and my horses do two to two and a half months before their first event at novice level. As the work increases so must the feed. The hard food has to be kept in proportion to the work. The work should include, if possible, trotting up hills and cantering on good going. If only small hills or banks are available, they can be used repetitively. If there are none, then longer work is needed. Cantering does not mean going flat out with the reins flapping; the horse should be going within himself, in balance and on the bit. To do this, the rider must keep the horse's head up, but without hollowing and stiffening the back, and have enough leg on the horse to ensure he is always taking a firm hold, as then the horse is less likely to injure himself.

It is helpful preparation for horse trials to do the odd dressage, jumping competition or hunter trials, and/or spend a winter hunting, the choice depending largely on the temperament and abilities of the individual horse, i.e. lazy horses benefit from hunting, temperamental ones from dressage. These are a useful means to find out about the tensions, pinpoint any problems and tackle them before having to put the phases all together in a horse trials.

On the day, the dressage and show jumping phases are tackled in the same way as at the specialist shows described above. The cross-country phase is similar to the jumping, other than the fact that the rider should take up the stirrups a few holes

to help give him more control when approaching fences at a faster speed. The principles are the same: balance, forward momentum and not being in a hurry to get to the fences. Those riders who ask for big stand-offs across country make heroes one week and hospital cases the next. The horses benefit from consistent training and riding. They are confused if one moment they have to stand off a fence, the next to trot and pop over one. The aim is to be going forward, with balance and rhythm; then the horse learns to wait, is more obedient and less mistakes are made.

One reason why I have had a certain amount of success is that I have always been short-sighted. As I was too self-conscious to wear glasses I often could not see from one fence to the next and could not read numbers. I had to walk the course very carefully and go from thistle to telegraph pole to

119 A last-minute check of a troublesome cross country fence

find my way around. It made me pay attention to detail when planning a cross-country course.

The major factor when crossing the country is to plan an exact line into, between and away from a fence. I picture in my mind how I will approach every fence in terms of speed and direction, and the way I am going to jump it. I always sit in the trailer before I start, and ride the course in my mind so that I know exactly at which thistle to slow down or speed up, where the going is slippery, deep or hard. In this way I anticipate nearly every eventuality.

On the course the most important thing is that when it comes to the last few strides the rider must be totally committed to going over the fence. Right or wrong the rider must keep the contact and keep kicking. It is surprising how a balanced, forward-going horse can get out of trouble, even when all seems lost!

If there is a hill, always sit quietly and try to gallop straight up or down, not along the side, as horses then tend to slip and hurt themselves. At the top the rider should sit still, allowing the horse to catch his breath before going on. Going downhill the rider needs to take extra care to keep his horse balanced. When jumping into a quarry, water, sunken road, coffin or from light to darkness, the horse needs time to see what he has to do. He can be ridden in strongly but not too fast. Parallels must be ridden straight, as this minimizes the spread, and the angle of a corner fence bisected and jumped at right angles (see diagram on page 86).

A rider should not be too proud to lean back over a drop fence and let the reins run through his fingers to prevent himself being pulled forward over the horse's head. When jumping into water the horse's or pony's head must be kept up with a

120 Jumping at speed in a Pony Club One Day Event

121 In order to take the shortest route the rider is taking the fence to one side and trying to turn the horse in the air

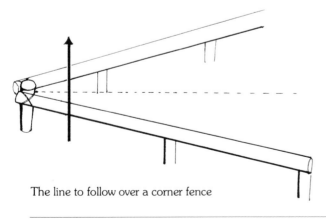

The line to follow over a corner fence

strong contact on the reins so that he lands with his front feet out in front of him; in this way the drag of the water does not make him lose his balance and fall forward in the following stride.

Finally, remember it is not clever to go faster than necessary since this puts more wear and tear on the horse or pony and exhausts him.

These are a few tips, but there is so much to be learnt about riding in equestrian events that in this book I have only been able to discuss the basic requirements. There is much more to cover and I shall do this in my next book on training for horse trials.

When competing, remember to have fun; horse and rider should enjoy themselves and prove the hours spent in preparation and training have made them into a good partnership.

PART 2
CARE OF THE HORSE

This second section is concerned with looking after the horse or pony (horse mastership).

It is a vital subject and anyone who is responsible for a horse or pony must master the basic facts as quickly as possible. I have written the section in note form to make it easier to get to the point and to provide quicker reference, and so that as much information as possible can be included in a small space.

11 · AT GRASS

Keeping a horse or pony at grass is far less time-consuming and cheaper than keeping it stabled. Apart from the lower cost of feed, bedding, buildings, overheads, etc. it also takes much less time to look after him and he does not have to be exercised every day. He will do enough moving around to keep healthy, and not be too fresh when ridden. It is difficult, however, to get a horse fit and muscular when he is kept out all the time. Also, although most ponies and some horses are sufficiently hardy to thrive outside all year round (if necessary with some hard feed and hay in winter), others lose condition rapidly when the grass has lost its goodness.

THE DAILY ROUTINE

1. Check to ensure the horses or ponies are healthy and sound, and have not been kicked or cut.
2. Feed if necessary. Those in regular work usually have to be fed, as do those who are losing condition.
3. Check the water supply, especially when frosty in winter.
4. Check the fencing and ensure there are no pointed, sharp objects which could cause damage.

FEET

The feet should be looked at regularly. Most ponies can be left fully shod, as they do little damage to one another in the field; but it is safest to take off the hind shoes of horses if they are turned out together, and this means the feet will be more liable to cracking and breaking. The blacksmith needs to trim unshod feet every six to eight weeks, and shoes must be removed and replaced before the feet grow too long. Most people leave on front shoes, even if the horse is not in work, to prevent the feet crumbling.

TEETH

These must be checked regularly, because if they become rough it is difficult for the horse or pony to eat. They need filing by the vet once or twice a year.

FENCING

The field must be safe for the horses and ponies, which means the fence must be high (over about 3ft 9ins) and strong enough to prevent them escaping. It should also be of a material which will not damage them if they run into or press against it.

Types of fencing

1. Post and rail is the best but also the most expensive. If horses start chewing it, run an electric fencing wire along the top rail.
2. Hedges are effective as long as they are thick and strong and have rails erected in weak areas. Beware of poisonous plants found in hedges such as yew and deadly nightshade – horses or ponies must not be turned out in fields where these occur.
3. Stone walls are effective but need to be kept in good order. A concrete coping prevents damage from water and rubbing by the animal.

4. Plain, heavy gauge wire between creosoted posts is relatively easy and cheap to erect. Three or four strands should be used. The lowest should be at least 1ft (30 cms) from the ground and all the wire must be kept taut to reduce the risk of injury.
5. Electric fencing. This is efficient and easy to move.

Fences to avoid

1. Barbed wire, especially if not taut.
2. Hurdles and chestnut paling.
3. Pig wire and sheep mesh.
4. Spiked iron railings.

The gate

This needs to be easy to open for humans but an effective barrier to horses. Well-fitted five-bar gates are best, but slip rails are a possibility.

WATER

Horses drink about eight gallons a day, so a constant supply of clean fresh water is needed.

Possible sources

1. An unpolluted stream but not a stagnant pond.
2. A self-filling water tank.
3. A tank or bath filled by a tap, though the tap should be covered so that the horse cannot hurt himself on it.

SHELTER

Horses and ponies need shelter in the winter from the wind, rain and cold, and in the summer from the flies. This can be obtained from:
1. The natural shelter of trees and high, thick hedges. These are usually sufficient except against the worst of the winter weather.
2. Sheds. These are best placed in the corner of the field with the open side facing away from the prevailing wind. It is important to have a wide entrance so that the horses and ponies do not get squeezed on entering and leaving or trapped inside.

GRASSLAND MANAGEMENT

Horses are choosy grazers, leaving patches of rough grass and cropping down the succulent areas. Their feet are heavy and quite large and poach wet ground. Their droppings restrict growth where they fall and also lead to infestation of the land with worm parasites (see page 113). For these reasons precautions need to be taken if the land is not to become 'horse sick'.

Precautions

1. Reasonable acreage. It is important that the fields are never grazed so bare that only the weeds and coarse grass thrive. It depends on the nature of the land and the size of the horses or ponies, but if they are out all year, one acre per horse is the normal minimum.
2. Alternative grazing. It helps to be able to put the stock into different paddocks, so it is better to have two or three small fields than a single large one.
3. Rotation. Ideally the land should be used for a sequence of different purposes. It can be rested, a hay crop can be taken, sheep may be put on it or, best of all, cattle. The latter eat the coarse grass, and the worm parasites that get into their system do not survive.
4. Removal of droppings. Daily removal is the best way of keeping the land sweet. Rotation and alternative grazing make this less necessary but if there is intensive use of the fields by horses, it becomes essential.
5. Harrowing helps to disperse the droppings and pulls out the matted growth of grass. It does not require a tractor, for a small harrow can be pulled behind a pony, Land Rover or even a car when the land is dry. The best time for harrowing is in the winter when the frost affects the droppings and kills the parasites. In summer harrowing spreads the dung but this tends to infect a larger area with parasites.
6. Topping. When cattle are not available to crop the long grass, topping (cutting the higher shoots) is advisable.
7. Rolling is useful, but not essential. Its particular value is if the weather (frost or heavy rain) or horses have disturbed the herbage and top soil.
8. Drainage helps to prevent poaching of the land. Sandy and chalky soils drain naturally, but on clay land artificial drainage is advisable as a long-term saving. Ditches around the field help provided they are kept clean, but pipe drainage is often worthwhile.

9. Fertilizers. Land constantly grazed by horses tends to become deficient in certain elements. A soil analysis can be done through the local department of agriculture, and then lime, phosphates, potash salts, nitrogen or basic manure added as advised.
10. Weeds. These flourish on overstocked, poached land. Buttercups and thistles can be sprayed in late spring, docks cut in July after flowering but before seeding, and ragwort sprayed in late spring. It is advisable to consult the local department of agriculture before spraying, and to check how soon after spraying the field may be grazed.

Poisonous plants

The following must be removed (check for the ones that are prevalent in your area):

1. Yew.
2. Ragwort, which is particularly dangerous when dead and therefore when present in hay.
3. Deadly nightshade, which is the most toxic, though woody nightshade can also cause poisoning.
4. Bracken, which can be dangerous to horses who have not developed an immunity to it. The rhizomes are more poisonous than the fronds, and this should be taken into account when ploughing re-claimed land.
5. Acorns and oak leaves, if eaten in large quantities.
6. Garden trimmings, which often contain toxic plants.
7. Water hemlock, found in marshes and damp places.
8. Spotted hemlock.
9. Laburnum, which is toxic, though fatal only in large amounts.
10. Potato stalks.

FEED

This will vary according to the condition of the stock, the time of year and the work they are doing. The grass is rich in spring and early summer but by autumn and through the winter it is little more than a bulk feed. Feed should be provided as soon as the stock starts to lose condition. For native or wild breeds this might not happen, but for refined breeds such as the Thoroughbred it can be for most of the year. To begin with hay can be given, but if this is not sufficient, then hard feed (oats, nuts, bran, etc.) must be provided in sufficient quantity to prevent the horse or pony losing condition.

Some ponies may become too fat on spring grass and be at risk to such problems as laminitis. Such ponies will either have to be put where there is less grass or shut in a stable for part of the day.

In winter check the condition of the horse by feeling his ribs, and do not be satisfied simply by looking at his long winter coat.

Feed utensils

Hay should be put in a haynet or hayrack to avoid wastage.

Hard feed is best put in a heavy round tin. Alternatively it is simple to make a utensil by cutting a tyre in half to make two complete circles and taking one and nailing it to a circular piece of wood.

HORSES IN WORK

Horses and ponies are often worked off grass, particularly children's ponies. This is successful if the following points are observed:

1. The work must be increased gradually. A horse or pony is not instantly fit if he has been living off the bulk feed of grass, especially in spring and summer.
2. Hard feed must be provided if the horse or pony loses condition and/or more energy is needed for the work.
3. The horse relies on the grease in his coat to keep him warm. Grooming removes this, so when it is cold he should only have the worst of the mud brushed off. Alternatively a New Zealand rug can be used. This rug is particularly secure and can be used on a horse who has been clipped when he is turned out.
4. Horses who sweat up when worked should be cooled down and not turned out until they are completely dry to avoid them developing colds or colic.

TURNING OUT

When a horse is first turned out after being stabled he can become very excited, gallop around and hurt himself. It is best to take him to the field on a lunge line, let him eat grass and become familiar with the wide open spaces before turning him loose.

12 · IN THE STABLE

Looking after a stabled horse is a big responsibility. He needs constant attention, a regular routine and daily exercise. It is not something to be undertaken lightly. Many people who have to stable a horse in order to keep him fit or because he loses condition at grass keep him at livery. This can be expensive but is fairer on the horse if the owner does not have the time to give him the necessary attention.

THE BUILDINGS

If you are building from scratch, careful planning will save much time in the future. Design a layout to minimize walking distances, e.g. bear in mind the proximity of water tap to horses, and of hay store and manure heap to stables.

Facilities needed

1. Stables.
2. Hay and bedding store.
3. Tack room.
4. Feed room.
5. Base for manure.

Constructions

1. Traditional – individual stables with door to outside, and separate units for storage, tack, etc.
2. Barn – all stables and units under one roof, with stable doors on to central passage. This version is time-saving and provides protection from the weather, but unless there are also outside doors to the stables there is an additional fire risk and the horses have a less interesting view.

Types of stable

1. Loose boxes, in which horses are free to move around, must be large enough (12ft × 10ft for a pony, 12ft × 14ft for a big horse), with walls free from protruding objects. The door must be at least 4ft wide, high and outward opening. It is normal for the door to be in two halves so that the upper part can be hooked back. Grills can be used on the upper half but I like my horses to see what is going on and not to be caged in. For the doors special bolts which horses cannot get caught on or open are best.
2. Stalls are smaller than loose boxes, and the horse is tied up by a rope or chain which is attached to his headcollar and runs through a ring or hole in the manger to a light weight resting on his bed. This system of tying up gives him the freedom for some movement and allows him to lie down. Cleaning out of stalls is much easier but the horses do get bored.

Fittings

1. Windows provide light but must be protected by grills.
2. Mangers should be fitted at about the height of the horse's chest and should be easy to clean out. If feed containers are placed on the floor or door, they should be removed as soon as the horse has finished his feed.
3. Fitted racks for hay are no longer popular as the dust falls in the horse's eyes. Instead, a ring about 5ft up is fixed to the wall and a haynet can be tied to this, high enough to prevent him putting his foot in it.

4. For water automatic bowls are labour saving but they tend to go wrong and need constant checking. A bucket container can be fitted on the wall but many people simply use a heavy bucket or container on the floor.
5. Although the haynet ring can be used for tying up, some people prefer to fit an additional ring.
6. Electric fittings must be out of reach of the horses or securely protected from them. Switches are best fitted outside the stable.

The floor

This should be hard-wearing, non-slip and impervious to moisture. It is best to have a slight slope towards a drain in a corner or outside the box.
Possible materials:

1. Concrete with a roughened surface.
2. Natural chalk soil.

Ventilation

It is important for the health of the horse to ensure there is fresh air but no draughts. The important points are:

1. Walls free from cracks and holes.
2. Windows hinged so that they open inwards from the top.
3. To provide warmth in winter it should be possible to shut the top doors and/or close up the barn.
4. To keep the horses cool in summer it should be possible to open the top doors and/or barn main doors.

NB For horses such as hunters who have to withstand wind and rain, many people keep the top doors open all year round.

The bedding

Whichever form of bedding is used it should provide insulation, encourage the horse to stale, prevent his feet being jarred and give him a bed to lie down on and rest.
Possible materials:

1. Straw. Wheat is the best type as horses tend to eat oat and barley straw; oat is more porous and barley can be prickly. Eating can be reduced by spraying the straw with disinfectant or stopped by muzzling the horse. Rotted straw is good for gardens, and mushroom farms in particular are keen to make use of it.
2. Peat is an expensive but effective form of bedding. It is easy to dispose of when rotted because of its value in the garden.
3. Shavings and sawdust are popular for bedding. Horses do not eat them and so they are better than straw for horses who have wind problems or allergy coughs, or who get too fat. Shavings are difficult to dispose of and most people keep their manure pile burning gently.
4. Shredded paper is the most dust-free bedding and is used for horses with serious allergy problems. It is expensive.

STABLE DUTIES

Tying up

Horses and ponies should be tied up whenever a person is working in the stable, grooming or saddling up. If left free, horses all too often kick, step on equipment or escape. Catch the horse, talk to him, put the rope of the headcollar around his neck, then the noseband over the muzzle and the headpiece over the ears before buckling it up.

A quick-release knot should be used for tying up to a small loop of string attached to the ring. The string will break if the horse panics and this will save him damaging himself by pulling the ring out or breaking the headcollar. The normal knot used is shown in the diagram.

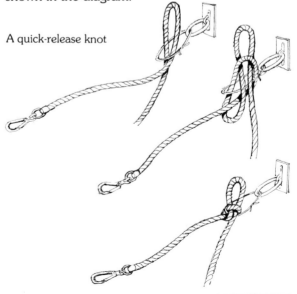

A quick-release knot

Mucking out

Utensils needed:

1. Wheelbarrow.
2. Shovel.
3. Broom.
4. Pitchfork (four blunted prongs for straw, six or more for shavings).
5. Skip (this can be a plastic laundry basket).
6. A sheet of sacking for carrying straw.
7. Rake for peat or shavings.

Aims

To keep the bedding clean, dry, thick enough to protect the horse from the floor and well banked up at the walls.

Procedure

For straw, pick up all droppings. Separate soiled bedding from clean with a pitchfork and heap the clean around the sides of the stable. The dung and wet straw is put on the sack, the floor brushed and allowed to dry before putting back the clean straw. The soiled bedding is taken to the manure heap. When necessary new straw can be added to the bed after the horse has been exercised. It must be well tossed.

For shavings, peat, sawdust and paper the droppings are collected into the skip or wheelbarrow, the bed forked, the wet removed and placed with the droppings. The soiled bed is then taken to the manure heap.

For all beds droppings should be removed throughout the day by putting them into the skip. Regular skipping out helps to keep the bed clean and makes mucking out easier. The day bed is normally kept thinner and the extra bedding banked up against the walls. In the afternoon the bed can be made thicker by adding more bedding and/or reducing the banks. This encourages the horse to lie down.

Deep litter

This saves time and money and is effective when there is good ventilation and drainage. The droppings are removed as frequently as possible and fresh bed laid on top. Gradually the bed gets deeper and when it reaches about 1 foot high it should be removed in its entirety (usually about every three to four months).

Rugging up

Stabled horses are often clipped out in winter and because they cannot move around much to keep warm they need protection. This is provided by rugs and blankets. There are many varieties on the market, from the inexpensive jute rug to various thermal types. The choice depends on the money available and how sensitive the horse is to the cold. It is advisable to keep horses in hard work as warm as possible without letting them break out into a sweat. The warmer the horses can be kept the less thick their coats grow, the less they sweat when exercised, and the less often they have to be clipped in winter. Those not in regular work and turned out should not be made too soft and reliant on being kept warm by luxurious rugs.

To put on a rug

Tie up the horse.

Take hold of the rug/blanket at the front and gently swing it over the horse's back so that it lies well forward, high up the neck.

Buckle the front.

Slide it back but not so far that it pulls tight on the shoulders and withers.

Fasten surcingles/straps if attached to the rug, otherwise place a pad over the saddle position and a roller over it. Check that the roller hangs flat, in the same position as the girth. Fasten the roller on the near side.

Run the fingers down the roller to smooth out any lumps in the rug.

Check that the rug fits, is neither too big nor too small around the horse's shoulders and is not dragging on the shoulders or withers. Sheepskin padding attached to the rug may be necessary to prevent pinching around the withers.

In cold weather a blanket is often worn under the rug. This is put on in the same way, lying well up the neck. Then, after the rug has been put on top of it and secured, the blanket lying up the neck is folded back over the rug to stop it slipping. The blanket should not lie further back than the root of the tail.

To take off the rug

Unfasten roller/surcingle, straps, etc.
Remove pad and roller.
Unbuckle the front fastening of the rug.

How to put a blanket on under a rug

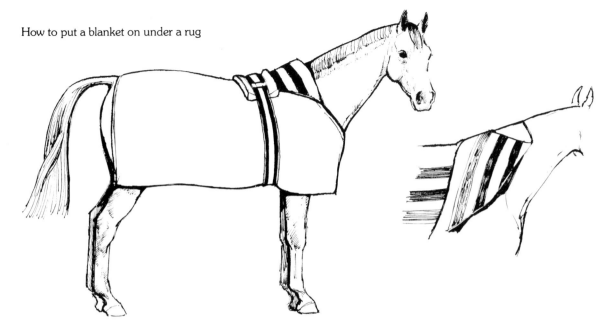

Fold back the front half of the rug (and blanket if used).

Hold the centre of the folded front of the rug with the left hand and the centre of the back with the right. Remove rug (and blanket) in a smooth backward sweep.

Rugs should be shaken daily to remove dust, sometimes hung out to air and about twice a year cleaned or washed. I have found that rugs kept in place with straps around the hindlegs, rather than a roller, suit my horses as they do not tighten over the wither or slip around.

BANDAGING

Types of bandage

1. Stable bandages are made of wool or stockinette and are about 4ins wide.
2. Exercise bandages are made of stockinette or slightly elastic material and are about 3ins wide. I find Velcro a safer fastening than tapes.
3. Tail bandages are made of stockinette or crepe and are about 2½–3ins wide.

Stable bandages

Stable bandages help to protect a horse's legs and keep them warm so their use is advisable on valuable animals or for those in a strange, small stable. They also help to reduce windgalls, particularly if used over Gamgee or light cotton sheeting soaked in witchhazel. Under normal conditions a horse should only need stable bandages when travelling.

To bandage

Care must be taken that the bandages are neither so loose they slip down nor so tight the hair becomes crinkled. Gamgee or special fibre helps to protect against the latter and is put on the leg over the area to be bandaged but with no edges over the tendons. Start bandaging below the knee or hock, taking the bandage around in even turns until it reaches the coronet, then work back up the leg and finish (see diagram on page 96). Fasten tapes in a bow, ensure they are flat and tuck in spare ends or secure by clip or Velcro. Any knot should be at the side of the leg.

To remove

Untie the tapes and unwind the bandage. Do not try to roll it up at the same time. Brush down hair that was covered by the bandage with the palm of the hand.

Exercise bandages

These are used for protection during exercise. They need to be applied with skill as they can cause damage if too tight or loose. Most people use boots except when a horse has a weakness in the limbs and/or needs extra protection.

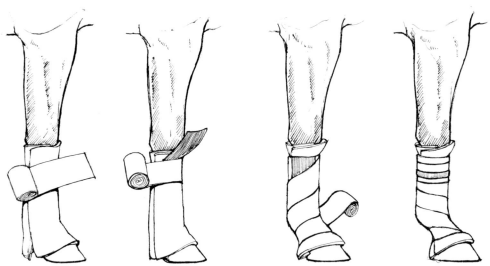

Putting on a travelling bandage

To bandage

Start at the side of the leg just below the knee or hock. Overlap each turn about 50 per cent so there is a double thickness all the way. Work downwards until the knuckle of the fetlock joint and then work back up.

The pressure should be kept even – not so loose as to slip, not so tight as to cut off circulation or restrict movement. Finish by folding over beginning of bandage and covering it, but taking care that fold is not at the back of the leg over the tendon.

Tie the tapes so that the knot of the bow is at the side and tuck the ends into the bandage. For competitions the tapes are usually stitched. Alternatively Velcro fastenings can be used.

Elasticated bandages can be used but with care as it is easy to put them on too tightly. Gamgee should be worn underneath and the person putting them on must appreciate that damage is easily done if they are too tight.

To remove

As for stable bandages.

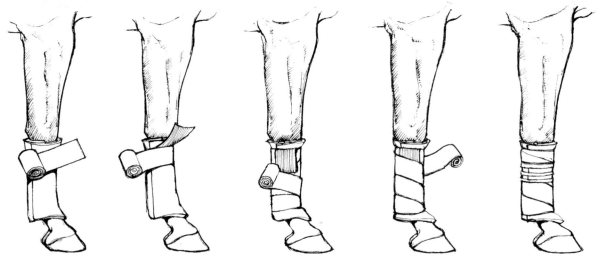

Putting on an exercise bandage

Putting on a tail bandage

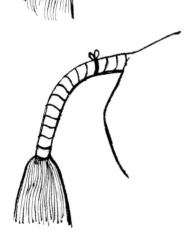

Tail bandage

This is used to make the tail lie better and for protection during travelling. It should not be left on for more than half a day as if it is tight enough to stay in place, it can cut off the circulation. It is not advisable to leave it on overnight.

To bandage

Dampen the tail with a water brush.
Hold the tail up with the left hand.
Unroll about 6ins of the bandage, place under the tail, hold it and the tail with the left hand while the right holds the roll of bandage. Turn the bandage around the tail securing the end. Make the second turn higher than the first and close to the dock. Then continue bandaging down the tail. Finish just before the last tail bone.
Tie the tapes neatly.

To remove

Untie the tapes. Take hold of the bandage with both hands and slide it down over the tail.

STABLE ROUTINE

Horses are creatures of habit. They relax if there is a routine and are disturbed by changes. The important factor is not what the routine is but to have a routine.

A typical programme

7.00 a.m.	Tie up, inspect for injuries, clear out any food left in manger, check for signs of ill health (see page 115).
	Adjust rugs.
	Clean water bucket, refill.
	Tie up small net of hay.
	Muck out.
	Untie.
7.45 a.m.	First feed.
9.30 a.m.	Tie up.
	Remove droppings.
	Remove rugs.
	Brush over.
	Pick out feet.
	Saddle up.
	Exercise.

10.30 a.m.	On return:		Untie.
	Tie up.		Second feed.
	Untack.	2.00 p.m.	General maintenance.
	Wash off feet.		Clean tack.
	Pick out feet.	4.30 p.m.	Tie up.
	Sponge off sweat marks.		Remove droppings.
	Rug up to keep warm. It is better for the horse to be too hot than too cold after exercise. Use a sweat rug if he has sweated and if the weather is cold this can be placed underneath another rug.		Pick out feet. Shake up bedding. Rug up with night rug(s)/blanket. Refill water bucket. Refill haynet.
	Untie.		Untie.
			Third feed.
Noon	Tie up.	7–9.00 p.m.	Tie up.
	Groom.		Remove droppings.
	Put on fresh rugs.		Refill water bucket.
	Refill water bucket.		Refill haynet (if necessary).
	Remove droppings.		Untie.
	Refill haynet.		Fourth feed (if necessary).

13·FEEDING

In his native state the horse eats small amounts throughout the day. His system cannot deal with spasmodic large feeds. Also his small long intestine is prone to getting food impacted, leading to the formation of gas and eventually colic. It is, therefore, important that he has a constant supply of fibre to prevent fermentation and compaction.

If he is in hard work, he will need protein to build up the muscles and repair damaged tissue, as well as carbohydrates for energy, and minerals and vitamins to maintain health.

TYPES OF FEED

Bulk feed

Bulk feed supplies the vital fibre that makes up the staple diet for stabled horses, providing between one half and two-thirds of their food.
1. Hay. The best type of hay is seed hay but other kinds are quite palatable as long as they are sweet smelling, free of dust, not too coarse and between about six and eighteen months old.
2. Haylage. This is a cross between hay and silage. It is particularly useful for horses who are allergic to hay and dust. It is high in protein but is expensive.

Concentrates/hard feed

These are given in addition to hay and never as a substitute. They must be introduced gradually and progressively since overfeeding, especially of proteins, can upset the metabolism.
1. Bran. Bulky and rich in proteins, it has relatively few energy-giving carbohydrates. If fed wet it acts as a laxative, if fed dry it tends to constipate.

2. Oats. These are the most effective energizers. They can be fed whole but are more digestible if crushed or bruised.
3. Barley is a good fattening food. It is best fed boiled but micronized flaked barley can be bought. The latter, if used, should be introduced very gradually to the diet.
4. Corn is high in energy value and has good fattening effects. It contains little protein and can be rather heating. It is fed flaked and should not make up more than one quarter of the grain ration.
5. Sugarbeet is usually bought dried as pulp and must be soaked in water for twelve hours prior to use. It is a good, relatively cheap conditioner, being high in carbohydrates.
6. Horse cubes or pellets are made up to provide a balanced diet. They can be the sole hard food used. Normal brands do not contain too high an energy value and so are good for ponies and spirited horses. Some types, e.g. racehorse cubes, are a good supply of energy.
7. Chaff is chopped hay and if added to the feed ensures healthy chewing of the concentrates.
8. Peas and beans are rich in proteins. They are fed split or crushed and are useful in small quantities for horses in hard work.
9. Root vegetables encourage poor feeders. Carrots are the best but turnips, swedes and indigenous beets are also useful in small quantities.
10. Molasses meal sprinkled on feed encourages finicky feeders and stimulates a shiny coat.
11. Cod liver oil helps to build up condition and a shiny coat. It does not taste good to horses, so more palatable substances are added to it and it is then sold under brand names.

12. Mineral salt licks or lumps of rock salt can be left in the manger or attached to the wall.
13. Linseed is a good conditioner but must be soaked and well cooked before feeding. It is a good addition to bran mashes.
14. Wheat except as bran is not suitable for horses.
15. Supplements are available in numerous forms. They are particularly useful for horses in very hard work or those recovering from an illness. If in doubt as to which one should be used, consult your vet.

Bran Mash

This is usually fed weekly on the night before a rest day and is especially beneficial after a hard day's work and before a rest day. To make the mash, half fill a bucket with bran, pour boiling water into it until it is completely saturated, add 1–4 oz salt or Epsom salts and a handful of oats or boiled barley. Cover with a sack and leave until cool enough to eat. A little soaked or cooked linseed can also be added.

PRINCIPLES OF FEEDING

1. Feed little and often. For horses in hard work four feeds a day are best.
2. Feed plenty of bulk, but only a small amount in the morning before exercise; give the major part in the evening haynet.
3. The amount of feed depends on:
   (a) The work being done.
   (b) The size of the horse.
   (c) The temperament of the horse.

Feeding chart

Type of Horse	Breakfast	Lunch	Tea	Supper
Hunter, or event horse over 16 hh	2 lb oats 1 lb bran + chaff 2 lb hay	3 lb oats ½ lb bran + chaff 5 lb hay	3 lb oats ½ lb bran roots, chaff 7 lb hay	4 lb oats 1 lb bran + chaff
Hunter, or event horse, under 16 hh	2 lb oats ½ lb bran + chaff 2 lb hay	3 lb oats ½ lb bran + chaff 4 lb hay	2 lb oats ½ lb bran, roots, chaff 6 lb hay	3 lb oats 1 lb bran + chaff
14.2 hh pony, hunting or eventing (turned out by day)	2 lb cubes ½ lb bran + chaff 2 lb hay	turned out	2 lb oats ½ lb bran + chaff 6 lb hay	2 lb oats 1 lb cubes 1 lb bran
Show jumper/dressage horse over 16 hh	2 lb oats ½ lb bran + chaff 2 lb hay	2 lb oats 1 lb cubes ½ lb bran + chaff 5 lb hay	2 lb oats ½ lb bran + chaff 7 lb hay	3 lb oats 1 lb cubes 1 lb bran + chaff
Riding horse of about 15 hh (turned out by night in summer or by day in winter)	1 lb oats 2 lb cubes ½ lb bran 2 lb hay	1 lb oats 2 lb cubes 1 lb flaked maize ½ lb bran + chaff 3 lb hay	2 lb oats 1 lb cubes ½ lb bran, roots 6 lb hay	
Child's pony of about 13.2 hh being worked daily (turned out by day)	1 lb cubes 1 lb bran 1 lb hay	2 lb cubes 1 lb bran 2 lb hay	1 lb oats ½ lb bran + chaff 1 lb carrots 5 lb hay	

(d) For horses at grass the weather and feed value of the grass.

(e) The condition of the horse.

4. Changes in feed (time or type) should be gradual and spread over a few days.

5. Dust is bad for horses; dampen the feed and avoid mouldy food-stuffs.

6. Work should not be done after a feed or if the horse's stomach is full of grass. Quiet work is possible soon after a very small feed, but no hard work should be done for one and a half hours after a full feed.

7. Water before feeding.

8. Clean all feeding utensils.

9. Oats are the main energizer. If a horse or pony becomes too fresh, reduce the quantity, substitute cubes and turn out the animal to grass. In most cases if the horse is too fresh it is important not to reduce the quantity of feed but simply to change the proportions.

SPECIMEN DIETS

Feeding is a skill requiring experience and observation. There are no hard and fast rules. The diets given are for typical animals but the skilled feeder will vary the amounts according to the horse's condition and energy. Feeding is judged by how a horse looks and behaves. If he looks well and goes well, the job is well done; if he is skinny or lazy, he needs more; if fat or fresh, he needs less in quantity or different food that is not so fattening or energizing.

WATERING

A supply of clean fresh water is vital to a horse's well-being.

Principles of watering

1. Before feeding, the horse must have the opportunity to drink. It is harmful to drink a large quantity on a full stomach.

2. The horse should not be allowed to drink much water before exercise.

3. After exercise the horse should be given water. If he is very hot, it is best to mix a little warm water with it to take off the chill. Do not give him more than half a bucket at one time. He should then be walked around so that he does not break out.

4. Water containers need frequent cleaning. Many horses will not drink dirty water.

Methods of watering

A constant clean supply is the aim.

1. Buckets. These are convenient and if made from plastic or rubber the horse cannot hurt himself on them. Most horses will need two. They can be put on the floor or in a bucket holder. They should be placed well away from the haynet and manger so that they do not get soiled by feed.

2. Automatic drinking bowls. These are labour-saving but some horses will not drink from them. They need constant checking as they become dirty and often fail to work.

3. For horses at grass the possible sources are discussed on page 90.

14·GROOMING

The main purpose of grooming is to keep the horse clean but it is also a form of massage which helps to tone up muscles and stimulate circulation. Grooming is essential to the well-being of a stabled horse but for the grass-kept horse it has to be limited, as the grease and dandruff help to waterproof the hair and keep him warm.

EQUIPMENT

Hoof pick

This is used to remove dirt and stones from the feet. The feet are picked up by running the hand down the back of the leg and if necessary pushing the horse's weight over on to the other fore or hind leg. The lifted foot is held in one hand and picked out with the point of the pick to remove stones, mud or bedding into a skip. Always work from the heel down towards the toe.

How to pick out a hoof correctly

123 Picking out the feet

124 The end of a stroke with the body brush by a very young groomer

Dandy brush

A stiff brush for the removal of mud and caked sweat. It is used on areas with thick hair and is too hard for tender regions or on a clipped or fine-coated horse. Grass-kept horses are groomed mainly with the dandy brush.

Body brush

Softer than the dandy brush, the body brush is used to remove dust and scurf and to brush the mane and tail. Short, circular, strong, but not thumping, strokes are taken with the body brush in the same direction as the hair lies. The head is brushed more gently, and after the headcollar has been removed and fastened around the neck. When using the body brush on the mane and tail, separate a few locks with your free hand and brush until tangle-free.

Curry comb

A metal curry comb is used for cleaning the body brush. It is held in the other hand to the body brush when grooming the body but is not used when body-brushing the head, mane or tail. The body brush is drawn through the comb after every three or four strokes over the body. The curry comb is cleaned by tapping it on the floor to remove the dust. A plastic or rubber curry comb (but not the metal version) can be used to remove caked mud and sweat or a moulting coat.

Water brush

A soft brush which is dipped in water and used to dampen the mane and tail, which are then brushed into the desired position. It is also used to wash the feet if they are dirty.

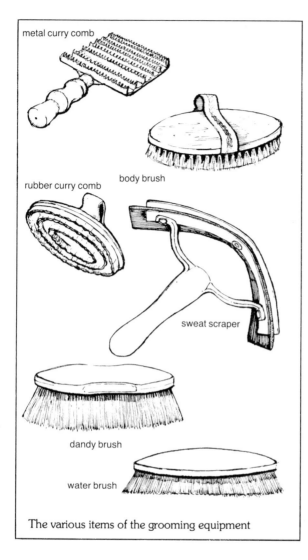

The various items of the grooming equipment

(labels within illustration: metal curry comb, body brush, rubber curry comb, sweat scraper, dandy brush, water brush)

Wisp

A twist of hay used to massage the horse and to develop the muscles. It should be slightly dampened, held in one hand and brought down with a thump on the horse in the direction of the lie of the hair. It can be used on muscular areas like the neck and quarters but not on bony prominences or sensitive regions such as the loins.

To make a wisp twist some hay into a rope, approximately 7 ft long. Dampen it and then form two loops at one end of the rope. Twist the rope around these loops as shown in the diagram. Finish by twisting the end through each loop and tucking it beneath the last turn. The finished wisp should be hard and firm and easily held in the hand.

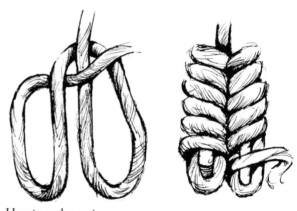

How to make a wisp

Box, wire basket or bag

One of these is needed in which to keep all this grooming equipment.

Grooming machine

A grooming machine can be helpful in a large stable. It must be used with care and according to instructions. It is important that the horse is introduced to it slowly and carefully.

THE GROOMING ROUTINE

In all grooming sessions the horse is tied up and the rugs removed.

Quartering

The first grooming session of the day is a quick one, to smarten up the horse before exercise. The feet are picked out; stable marks are cleaned first

Sponges

A damp clean sponge is used to clean dirt from around the eyes and muzzle and another sponge for the dock region under the tail.

Stable rubber

A cloth which when arranged into a bundle is used to give the coat a final polish in the direction of the hair.

Sweat scraper

This is used to remove water and sweat from the coat by literally scraping it gently along the wet coat in the direction of the hair.

with a dandy brush then with a damp sponge; the mane and tail are brushed with a body brush then dampened into place with a water brush; the eyes, muzzle and dock are sponged.

After exercise

Feet are picked out and can be washed off, but in cold weather it is best only to wash them when they are very dirty. Dry sweat marks are removed with a dandy or body brush. If the sweat is still wet, the horse can be sponged down with tepid water and the sweat scraper used. Then the horse is walked around until he is dry, preferably wearing a sweat rug. It is easy for a stabled horse to chap and develop sores when his coat gets wet, so he must be well dried, particularly over the sensitive parts and areas of pink skin.

Strapping

This is the thorough grooming of the day. Again the feet are picked out; then the dandy brush is used with a to-and-fro motion wherever there is caked mud or sweat. With sensitive horses and those who are clipped, it is often better to use a rubber curry comb for this work. Body brushing is the major part of strapping and this is the hardest work, as the strokes should be strong and have the weight of the person behind them. It helps to hold the brush in the left hand on the nearside and right on the off side. The whole body is brushed, starting with the neck and progressing to the hind legs (stand close to the horse at his side when brushing the latter, then if the horse tries to kick, there will be little strength behind any blow). Finish with the head. The mane and tail are brushed and dampened. The tail can be bandaged. The eyes, muzzle and dock are sponged and the horse wiped over with a stable rubber. The feet are picked out and hoof oil is applied to the outer surface. For horses who have to be in top condition or those who need to build up muscles then wisping is useful and is done after the body brushing.

Setting fair

Most horses have their rugs changed and straightened at the end of the day and this is an opportunity to give them a final brush.

15 · CLIPPING, TRIMMING AND PLAITING*

Clipping is the removal of all or part of a thick coat.

Reasons for clipping

1. To reduce sweating, so that a horse is less likely to lose condition and can carry out faster and longer work.
2. To enable a horse to dry off more quickly.
3. To save labour on grooming.
4. To make a horse look neat and smart.

Equipment

1. Hand clippers – inexpensive but very slow.
2. Wheel machine clippers – old-fashioned.
3. Electric clippers.

Care of clippers

1. They must be well oiled before and during clipping.
2. Blades must be sharp – if blunt they pull the hair.
3. They should be kept as cool as possible during clipping, so keep them clean with a brush, and oil them frequently. If necessary, strip, clean and wait to cool.
4. Always clean well after use.

Principles of clipping

1. Be patient and take time to introduce the horse to the machine. Start by simply letting him hear the noise, then put the clippers on to his body but do not clip; only after this goes smoothly should you begin the clipping.

2. A clean, dry coat is the easiest to clip.
3. Start with easy regions, e.g. the shoulders.
4. The most sensitive areas are the head, flank and belly; an assistant can lift one of the horse's legs to prevent him moving around.
5. The blades should be applied against the lie of the coat and should be parallel to the coat so they do not dig into the skin.
6. Hair should not be removed from the insides of the ears.
7. Care is needed to clip a straight line along the crest of the neck and not into the mane.
8. To keep the horse as relaxed as possible let him eat from a haynet, and have an assistant available to hold and calm him if necessary.
9. Whenever possible, put a rug over the clipped area to keep him warm.
10. In areas where the skin wrinkles, e.g. the elbows, pull it taut before trying to clip.
11. If the horse is difficult a twitch can be used.

A twitch

*In USA and certain other countries, plaiting is termed braiding

Types of Clip

The type of clip depends on the work to be done and whether the horse is stabled or put out to grass wearing a New Zealand rug.

1. Full clip – all the coat is removed.
2. Hunter clip – all the coat, except that on the legs downwards from the elbow or top of the second thigh, and under the saddle.

A hunter clip

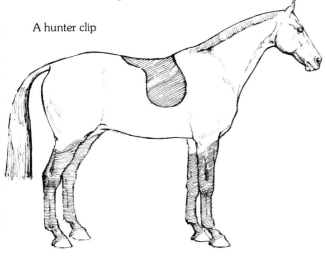

3. Blanket clip – the coat is removed from the head, neck and belly, but left in the shape of a blanket on the back, as well as on the legs.

A blanket clip

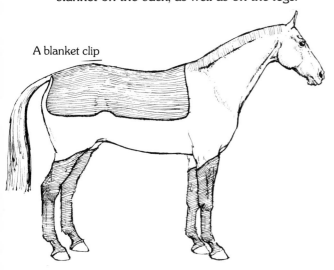

4. Trace-high clip – hair is removed only from part of the thighs, belly and chest and sometimes the under part of the neck. This is used for horses who go out to grass and for harness horses (the clip is up to the level where traces run – hence its name).

A trace clip

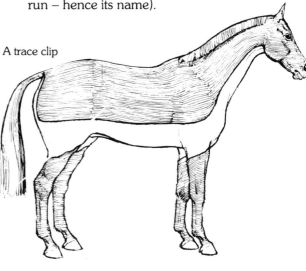

TRIMMING

This is the removal of hair – mainly from the mane, tail, heels and chin – to tidy up the horse.

Pulling the mane

This is done to thin out and shorten the mane.

1. Try to ensure the horse is warm, as his pores are then open and hairs come out more easily.
2. Brush the mane.
3. Pull a few hairs at a time with fingers or by winding them around a mane comb and plucking out sharply. Do not try to pull out too many hairs at a time as this will be painful to the horse and unsettle him.
4. Only take hairs from the underside of the mane.
5. Do not pull for too long. It is better to have a number of sessions rather than make the horse sore and upset.

Hogging

The whole of the mane is removed with clippers.

1. An assistant holds the horse's two ears and keeps the head down so that the crest is stretched.
2. Clippers are used to remove the mane from the withers to the forelock.

Pulling the tail

A tail can be left unpulled but then it will need plaiting for special occasions.

1. Brush the tail in the dock area.
2. Pull hairs from the dock region, starting with the hair underneath and progressing to hairs on the sides.
3. Pull both sides evenly.
4. Start at the top and work down, stopping before the end of the tail bone; the length pulled can be according to taste.
5. Only pull a few hairs at a time.
6. As for the mane, it is best to do a little bit each session, especially with horses who become restless.
7. The pulled tail can be bandaged for three or four hours.

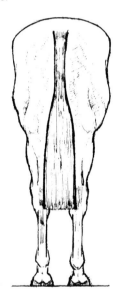

A pulled tail

Cutting

A number of areas look better if hairs are cut.

1. Tail – the length of the tail varies according to taste but most people like their horse's tail to be cut straight along the bottom, whether it is nearly on the ground or up to about 4 ins below the point of the hock.
2. Legs – if these are not clipped, excess hair at the back is cut off with scissors. The mane comb is run up through it, against the lie of the coat, and the hair cut off.

3. Poll – it is usual to cut a small area of the mane where the headpiece of the bridle sits.
4. Withers – the mane is usually cut over these, as long hairs tend to get rubbed off by rugs and numnahs.
5. Whiskers – long whiskers are usually cut off. These are quite numerous around the chin.

PLAITING THE MANE

This is done to make a horse look smart and to train the mane to stay on the required side.

With thread

1. Collect: a water brush; 8 ins lengths of strong thread the colour of the mane; a needle with a large eye; a mane comb and a pair of scissors.
2. Dampen the mane with the water brush.
3. Divide the hair into the desired number of sections with mane comb. It is usual to have an uneven number of plaits on the neck, plus the forelock. Hunters have a minimum total of six plaits; and the fashion for show jumpers and dressage horses is to have a large number.

4. Plait the first section tightly and, when three parts of the way down, plait in a piece of doubled-over thread. When the plait is finished wind the thread around the plait and pull tight.

5. Complete all the plaits and if one is much longer than the others, double it under.

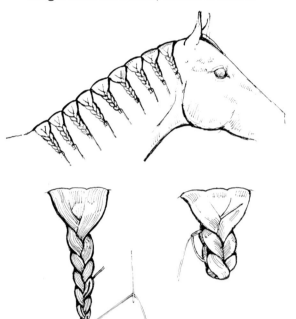

6. Thread the needle through the two ends of cotton, double over the plait and pull the needle through from underneath close to the crest. Pull the thread through.

7. Remove the needle and bind the thread tightly around the plait before knotting underneath; cut off the ends of the thread.

With rubber bands

Plait as before and wind the elastic band several times round the end of the plait before doubling over the plait and winding the band around the entire plait until tight.

PLAITING THE TAIL

1. Brush and dampen the tail.

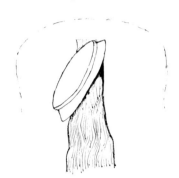

2. Start plaiting at the top, taking a small section of hair from the centre and from either side.

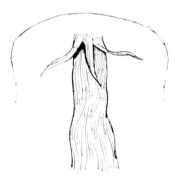

3. Continue plaiting down, drawing in further sections from the sides.

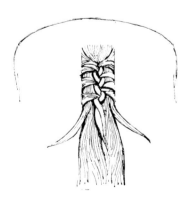

4. When about two thirds of the way down the tail bone, stop using side hair.

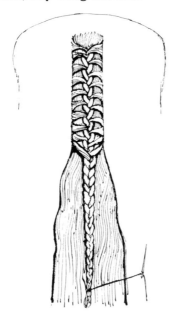

5. Continue plaiting the centre hairs and when finished stitch and bind before doubling over the plait and attaching to the point where side hairs were no longer used.

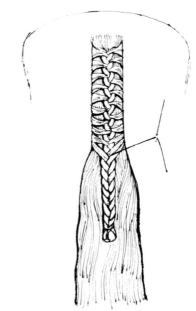

16 · CARE OF TACK

Care of tack is an essential part of looking after the horse. Broken tack can cause accidents; ill-fitting equipment may result in injuries and sores.

Routine

1. Clean all saddlery after use.
2. Inspect all tack at regular intervals (weekly if the horse is exercised daily) to check stitching and leather for signs of wear, and bits for any roughness. Dismantle the tack for this check and then clean it, using saddle oil if the leather is dry, before putting it together again.

CLEANING TACK

Equipment

1. Sponge/towelling for washing.
2. Chamois leather for drying.
3. Sponge for saddle soap.
4. Saddle soap.
5. Saddle oil.
6. Metal polish.
7. Stable rubber to dry metalwork.
8. Dandy brush to remove mud and sweat from linen linings, webbing girths, etc.
9. Duster to polish metal.
10. Bucket.
11. Bracket on which to hang tack.

To clean

Leather

1. Dampen with warm but not hot water. Do not soak leather to clean it.
2. Dry naturally or with chamois leather.

3. Dip bar of saddle soap into water and then rub into a dry sponge; or, if you have a tin of saddle soap, use a very lightly dampened sponge to apply soap.
4. Do not put leather too near to a fire or any heat; do not get leather too wet.

Linen

Brush, sponge or scrub, then dry.

Serge

Brush, and only when essential scrub, as it takes time to dry.

Metal

Wash, dry, apply metal polish, then polish.

Nylon or webbing girths

Brush and when necessary wash and rinse.

The saddle

1. Dismantle, including taking irons off leathers.
2. Clean lining.
3. Stand up to dry.
4. If possible, put on saddle horse.
5. Clean all leather, particularly the undersides of the flaps.
6. Occasionally a proprietary brand of oil should be used on undersides of flaps but not on seat.
7. Clean metal work.
8. Clean girth according to material.

Numnahs and saddlecloths

1. Brush after use.
2. Clean regularly, according to material.
3. Check wear. Many saddlecloths get nobbly after numerous washings.

Boots

1. Brush daily.
2. Clean by washing/saddle soaping, according to materials.

Bridles

Daily cleaning

1. Hang up on hook.
2. Check noseband and throatlash are undone.
3. Take straps out of keepers but leave buckled up.
4. Wash bit (but not leather) in bucket.
5. Wash leather but only by dampening, not soaking.
6. Dry, if necessary, with chamois leather.
7. Polish bit and buckles.
8. Soap leather.

Thorough cleaning

1. Undo all buckles, noting in which holes the buckles were fastened.
2. Wash leather.
3. Soap and/or oil leather.
4. Put together.

Martingales, neck straps

As for leather.

Clothing

Rugs, blankets and bandages need the dust shaken out of them regularly. According to material, they can be washed or dry cleaned when they become dirty.

Looking after tack

1. Never drop a saddle.
2. Hang saddle and bridle in the tack room as shown in the photographs.
3. To carry a saddle:
   (a) place the front arch in the crook of the elbow or
   (b) press the cantle into the waist and support the front arch with the hand.

125 The snaffle bridle correctly hung up

126 The double bridle correctly hung up

4. To stand a saddle:
   (a) stand it on its front arch on the folded girth so that the pommel is not scratched or
   (b) lean it against the wall with the girth coming under the arch and then up over the cantle to prevent its being scratched by the wall or
   (c) place it on the ground with the flaps out in the same position as when on the horse's back.

17 · MAINTENANCE OF HEALTH

WORMS

These intestinal parasites are a major hazard in the care of horses. They can cause colic, loss of condition and even death.

Prevention

1. Regular worming with worm powders/pastes as advised by vet. Horses at grass need them about every six weeks, stabled horses before and after being turned out to grass for their holiday, plus bi- or tri-monthly doses. In addition occasional worm counts (by the vet) are advisable. Sometimes the wormers are ineffective and a stomach pump is necessary.
2. Care for pastures (see page 90) to ensure they do not become horse sick.

TEETH

These can wear unevenly and so develop sharp edges. Also some teeth may need removing. Either of these problems will make the mouth sore and the horse will tend to become a finicky feeder and/or hard to get to accept a bit when ridden.

Prevention

Annual or bi-annual checks by the vet. Our horses are looked at at least twice a year.

FEET

Care of the feet is vital to the well-being of the horse. Badly shod, poorly shaped or injured feet are the most common causes of lameness.

The structure of the foot is seen in the diagram. The outer surface – comprising the wall, sole and frog – are non-sensitive, so they can be pared back and nails can be inserted into the wall without causing pain. The wall is the visible surface growing down from the coronet. The sole protects the foot from injury from below and the frog is an anti-slipping shock absorber.

Since horses in work tend to wear the horn away, most are shod. As the shoe protects the wall, which is continuously growing, the foot will become very long if neglected. Regular shoeing is vital at intervals of four to six weeks. We shoe ours about once a month, depending on the amount of roadwork they are doing.

Annotated diagram of foot

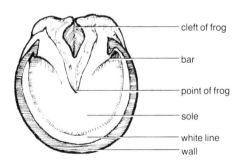

- cleft of frog
- bar
- point of frog
- sole
- white line
- wall

Signs that shoeing is needed

1. Shoe is loose.
2. Shoe is worn thin.
3. Clenches are risen (nails stand out from wall).
4. Foot is long.
5. Shoe has been lost.

Types of shoeing

1. Hot shoeing, in which the shoe is heated and moulded to fit the foot. This ensures the best fit.
2. Cold shoeing, in which a ready-made shoe is fitted to the foot.

Types of shoe

1. Plain stamped – shaped bar of iron.
2. Hunter shoe – concave iron, with groove (fullered) to provide more grip.
3. Feather-edged – inner branch feathered to reduce risk of brushing opposite leg.
4. Grass tip – half-length shoe for horses at grass to prevent splitting of wall around toe.
5. Surgical shoes – specially designed to assist with injury, conformation or disease.
6. Racing plates – light fullered shoes, usually made of aluminium.

Studs

To reduce slipping, studs can be worn. Special road studs can be kept in permanently but larger ones are screwed into a stud hole in the shoe as needed.

Studs come in various lengths and sizes to suit the different going. In deep going a big blunt stud is needed, in hard ground a short pointed one. When a stud is removed the holes are blocked with cotton wool to prevent clogging. A metal 'tap' can be used to clean out the holes.

Checks on new shoes

1. Type of shoe is suitable for work.
2. Weight of iron proportional to size of horse.
3. Shoe fits foot, not vice versa with severe paring of foot.
4. Frog in contact with ground.
5. Adequate number of nails used, usually three on inside and four on outside.
6. Clenches neat and in line.
7. No space between shoe and foot.
8. Shoes not too narrow at the heel.
9. Pastern and wall of hoof are in a continuous line. There is no angle between them, no break at the coronet which would restrict the blood supply to the hoof.

For a well-shod foot, see Chapter 2, photograph 12.

18 · COMMON AILMENTS

The following outline is intended to explain to the horse owner the symptoms of serious problems; the symptoms and treatment for the more straightforward ones, and the precautions that can be taken against incurring any problems.

When a horse or pony becomes ill or lame there are a number of simple solutions, discussed below; but if these are not effective, or if the indications are that the problem is serious or there is any uncertainty about diagnosis, then call the vet.

SIGNS OF ILLNESS

1. Horse leaves feed.
2. Horse gets thin and 'tucked up' (back part of abdomen shrinks upwards).
3. Droppings are not passed, or are passed less often, or consistency changes, or mucus or parasites are visible. Droppings should consist of round balls which break on hitting the ground.
4. Dull eyes and glazed expression.
5. Discharge from eyes and/or nostrils.
6. Swollen legs.
7. Coat is dull, starey and/or tight. Horse starts to sweat.
8. Temperature above/below the normal of 37.8°C (100–101°F).
9. Breathing abnormal or restricted, or respiratory rate quickens (normal is 10–15 breaks per minute – count by watching flank rise and fall).

TO TAKE THE TEMPERATURE

1. Lubricate thermometer with oil or soap.
2. Have the horse held by an assistant.
3. Raise tail and insert thermometer into rectum so that it touches the side. Keep hold of thermometer until removal.

WOUNDS AND INJURIES

To stop bleeding

If necessary apply pressure bandage.

To clean

If necessary cut away surrounding hair. Trickle cold water from a hosepipe or bathe with cotton wool soaked in salt and water (1 teaspoon salt to 1 pint of water), or in 1 part hydrogen peroxide to 10 parts warm water. Harsh antiseptics or disinfectants are not advisable. Do not probe puncture wounds, leave this to a vet.

To dress

Apply antibiotic powder or a healing cream. Then put lint, followed by cotton wool, followed by bandage, over wound. If it is a bruised wound, then the dressing can be a poultice, Animalintex if it is open, Kaolin if it is not.

Call vet

(1) if stitching is needed; (2) if it is a puncture, as antibiotics are usually needed; (3) if anti-tetanus is not up to date; (4) if there are any signs of infection – swelling, refusing food, beginning to sweat.

Special types of wounds

Girth galls (rubs by the girth) – use fomentations until healed then apply salt and water or surgical spirit to harden. Avoid using saddle for a few days then use a string girth or a sheepskin tube over the girth.

Saddle sore – do not use saddle until healed. If ill-fitting saddle caused it, ensure this is corrected. Harden sore as for girth galls.

Broken knees (cut knees) – call vet if wound is deep, otherwise treat with slow trickle of water from hosepipe. Apply Animalintex poultice. Bandage with criss-crossing behind the knee initially. Then use surgical stocking attached to Elastoplast above the knee and dressing under it.

LAMENESS

1. A horse shows his lameness most obviously at a trot going downhill.
2. Decide which leg he is reluctant to put weight on and which is causing the problem.
3. Start by inspecting the foot and pick out to ensure no stone, nail, etc, is causing the pain.
4. Examine the foot and leg for heat, swelling and any painful area.
5. Call the vet if there is any difficulty in identifying the problem or if there are signs of infection.
6. Alternatively a blacksmith may be needed if the problem is in the foot, and the shoe needs removing and the foot paring.
7. If horse is stabled and cannot be worked because of the lameness, feed a laxative diet of bran mash, see page 100.

Types of treatment

Hot Fomentation

This is of value when it is difficult to poultice.

Method
1. Half fill a bucket with water which is hot but does not scald the hand.
2. Add a handful of Epsom salts.
3. Immerse two pieces of thick cloth (can be a blanket or towel) about 2ft square in the water.
4. Take out one piece, fold it, squeeze out some water, hold over damaged area.
5. Replace with other piece of cloth as it cools and place original piece in bucket.

6. Top up water in bucket with hot as it cools.
7. Repeat, keeping injury hot for at least 20 minutes.

Poulticing

There are a number of poultices on the market but the best known are:

1. Kaolin – used for inflammation and bruising.
   (a) Heat Kaolin in a tin in a pan of water (NB do not close lid as it may then explode).
   (b) Take a piece of cloth, Gamgee, cotton sheeting or brown paper and spread heated Kaolin on to it with a knife. Alternatively, spread Kaolin on to brown paper and place a piece of gauze over Kaolin. Heat under grill until so hot it can just be stood by back of hand. Apply as before.
   (c) Apply to sprain or bruise, then a piece of waterproof material and surround with cotton wool or Gamgee. Finally wrap around a bandage.
   (d) Re-apply twice a day.
       NB Kaolin can be used cold, for example on bruises.

2. Animalintex – this has excellent drawing qualities.
   (a) Cut poultice to size required.
   (b) Place on metal tray with slimey side up.
   (c) Pour over boiling water.
   (d) Squeeze out until you can touch Animalintex with back of hand without being scalded.
   (e) Apply with slimey side on to injury, in same way as for Kaolin.

3. Bran and Epsom Salt Poultice – this is used most often on the foot after the shoe has been removed.
   (a) Apply vaseline over heel to help stop it cracking.
   (b) Heat up bran mash, adding a handful of Epsom salts.
   (c) Put mash in a plastic bag.
   (d) Pick up foot and put in bag so that bran surrounds foot.
   (e) Put on poultice boot or piece of sacking secured around the pastern with string threaded through it. Bandage over the sack.

FLU VACCINATION

The flu vaccination is becoming compulsory in many competitive spheres. An initial primary shot has to be followed (usually within 90 days) by a secondary, another at six months then by annual boosters. It is best to get the vet to give these before a rest as a horse needs three to seven days of non-strenuous work following their injection. Regulations regarding vaccinations change and should be checked.

INSURANCE

Most owners like to insure their horse. There are many options:

1. Death from accident.
2. Death from accident, illness or disease.
3. Death from accident, illness or disease, or loss of use.
4. Veterinary fees.
5. Loss by theft or injury.
6. Loss of tack, or combination of the above.

The premium will depend on the policy, the use of the horse and its age. It is a good idea to get quotes from a number of companies as these can vary considerably.

FIRE PRECAUTIONS

Horses are terrified of fire and will not move towards it. If there is a fire, place a damp (if possible) rug or jacket over the horse's head and lead him to safety.

Precautions

1. Do not smoke in stables or horse boxes.
2. Ensure there are fire extinguishers in the stables and horsebox.

VICES

These are habits which are sufficiently serious to be considered unsoundnesses.

Weaving

Horse swings head, neck and sometimes shoulders from side to side, usually over the stable door.

Remedies

1. Since it can be caused by boredom, give more exercise and/or turn out to grass.
2. Hang two tyres on string from the top of the door frame so that horse will hit one tyre, then the other, as he swings.
3. Various metal frames can be bought specifically designed to be fitted as a top door for weavers.

Crib-biting and windsucking

Cribbers grip objects with their teeth and then suck in air. Windsuckers suck in air without catching hold of an object.

Remedies

1. More exercise and/or turn out to grass.
2. Provide a constant supply of hay and/or salt lick in stable so horse has something to do.
3. Paint the objects which he catches on to with anti-chew mixture.
4. Use a muzzle or cribbing strap.
5. Operation to remove relevant muscles from the throat.

NB   Horses sometimes copy each other, so those who weave or crib should be kept out of sight of horses free from such vices.

FIRST-AID EQUIPMENT

Thermometer.
Blunt surgical scissors.
Calico bandages, 2 ins and 5 ins wide.
Cotton wool.
Packet of lint.
Roll of Gamgee or cotton.
Cough expectorant.
Colic drink.
Glycerine.
Antibiotic powder.
Iodine.
Animalintex.
Kaolin.
Epsom salts.
Surgical spirit.
Antiseptic shampoo.
Antiseptic spray.
Kidney powders.

Common Ailments: Diagnosis, Treatment and Prevention

Problem	Symptom	Treatment	Prevention
Cold	Thin nasal discharge.	Keep warm. Call vet if condition deteriorates.	Do not subject to extremes of temperature.
Broken wind	Cough. When exhales exaggerated movement and flank heaves twice.	Incurable unless an allergy. Helped by keeping on dust-free diet and bed. Damp feed, soak hay or use haylage, paper bed or shavings. Keep in regular fast work.	Avoid dusty food and environment.
Whistling	High-pitched noise when breathing in.	Vet can tube or hobday.	Can be hereditary.
Flu	Usually temperature rises. Horse shows signs of illness.	Isolation, warmth, veterinary treatment.	Vaccination.
Virus	Off colour, loss of appetite. Positive confirmation usually only possible after blood test.	Take out of work; give tempting food, veterinary tonics.	
Strangles	Temperature, nasal discharge, swollen glands under jaw.	Call vet. Isolate. Keep warm. Long convalescence.	
Azoturia	Stiffness, staggering, sweating. If urine is passed it is brownish.	Call vet. If occurs when riding, keep warm, arrange for transportation back to stables.	Make sure diet is in proportion to work. Feed mash night before day off.
Tetanus	Stiffness, third eyelid flickers across eye, horse loses co-ordination.	Call vet. Darken stable, give laxative feed, plenty of water.	Vaccinate.
Colic	Paws ground, tries to roll, lies down, gets up, looks at belly, starts to sweat.	Give colic drink (should be kept with first-aid equipment). Keep horse walking around or, if put back in box, keep constant watch. If it does not improve within three-quarters of an hour of giving drink, call the vet.	Avoid dramatic change of diet. Take care when introducing new hay or turning out to spring grass. Always feed mash night before day off.

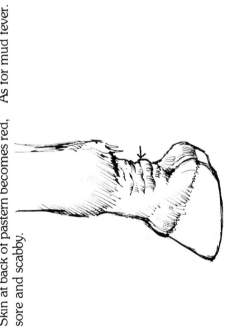

Ailment	Symptoms	Treatment
Ringworm	Small round hairless patches.	Isolate. Call vet. Treat accordingly. As is very contagious use separate grooming kit. Disinfect any clothing or part of body which comes in contact with victim.
Lice	Itchiness, small patches which horse keeps rubbing.	Clip horse. Use lice powder or wash. Cleanliness.
Sweat itch	Horse rubs off hair on dock and mane.	Do not turn out in sun or in early evening. Various lotions prescribed by vet. Dab dry, not rub dry. Protocon.
Mud fever	Skin rough, scabby and sore on limbs and occasionally belly. Some swelling.	Keep limbs dry. If they get wet, dry thoroughly, but by dabbing not rubbing. Apply soothing cream such as lanolin, Protocon or zinc ointment or as prescribed by vet. Do not ride or turn out where it is muddy.
Warbles	Small lumps, usually under saddle. (Don't confuse with blocked sweat glands or a heat rash).	Do not try to remove; allow to bore its way out, and apply iodine or antibiotic powder. Keep saddle off bump – if necessary, cut hole in numnah.
Cracked heels	Skin at back of pastern becomes red, sore and scabby.	As for mud fever. As for mud fever.

Condition	Symptoms	Treatment	Prevention/Cause
Constipation	Droppings not passed regularly, becoming harder than normal.	Bran mash, grass, Epsom salts in food or water.	
Worms	Loss of condition, bowel movement tends to be irregular, in severe cases colic.	Worm powder/paste from vet. Stomach pumping by vet.	Regular doses of wormer, grassland management so paddocks do not become horse sick.
Diarrhoea	Loose droppings.	Dry bran or Kaolin with food. Feed hay not grass.	Take care when putting on to spring grass.
Pricks and punctures	Pain/heat/swelling confined to small area.	Remove cause if still there, scrape hole to release pus. Poultice or put foot in bucket of warm salty water for 20 minutes several times a day.	Ensure blacksmith is high class, as often caused by nails in shoe.
Laminitis	Pain, reluctant to move and flinches when foot/feet are tapped. Stands with weight on heels. Ridges may appear in hoof.	Call vet. Remove shoes.	Usual cause is excess rich food. Avoid feeding too much barley/maize and do not allow horse to have too much spring grass.
Pedal ostitis	Trotting with short strides. Heat in foot. Confirmed with X-rays	Turn out on soft ground. Corrective shoeing.	Do not ride hard on firm surfaces.
Thrush	Unpleasant odour from cleft of foot.	Wash out foot thoroughly. If severe, start by poulticing, then apply Stockholm tar. In milder cases just tar.	Keep bed clean and pick out feet regularly.

	Symptoms	Treatment	Prevention
Bruised sole	Sole tender when pushed or banged with hammer.	Rest.	Leather pads on horses with thin soles.
Navicular	Intermittent lameness. Usually points affected toe in stable. Confirmation by X-ray.	Vet can prescribe treatment. Corrective shoeing.	Avoid excessive concussion to foot. Ensure horse is shod correctly with not too long a toe and the pastern and hoof at the same angle, i.e. no break at the coronet.
Splint	Bony enlargement on cannon bone. Starts quite small but horse will flinch if it is pushed.	Rest, blistering, pin-firing.	Wear boots; caused by blows or excessive work on immature limbs.
Bog spavin	Soft swelling on front and inner side of hock. Rarely heat or lameness.	Cold treatment, massage, astringents can help. If horse goes lame, rest and obtain advice from vet.	Avoid excessive work with young horses, especially if they have weak hocks.

Bone spavin	Bony enlargement on lower and inner side of hock. Lameness tends to wear off with work. May drag that toe (seen by wear on shoe).	Rest, sometimes blistering and pin-firing help; surgery.	Avoid excessive work with young horses, especially if they have weak hocks.
Curb	Enlargement below point of hock. Seen as a curve when viewed from side. Rarely causes lameness.	Rest if horse becomes lame, and obtain advice from vet.	Avoid excessive work with young horses, especially if they have weak hocks.
Gravel	Heat and swelling from foot upwards.	Find source of infection in foot. Vet or blacksmith to pare back. Usually he can release pus but, if deep, foot may need poulticing before and after pus is released. Antibiotics are usually advisable.	Frequent picking out of hooves so gravel or foreign object does not get lodged in foot.

Thoroughpin	Small swelling above and in front of point of hock. Rarely lame.	Very rarely a problem but rest, massage, astringents and in severe cases blistering help. Veterinary advice.	Avoid putting strain on young horse's hocks.
Corns	Bruises to sole around heels which get sorer with work.	Vet or blacksmith needs to remove shoe, pare back sole to find red spot of bruise. Then can poultice.	Careful shoeing to avoid pressure on seat of corn. Frequent shoeing so hooves do not grow too long.
Sprained fetlock joint	Heat, swelling, lameness.	Alternate hosing with cold water and hot Kaolin poultice. Rest. Gradual reintroduction to work.	Avoid jarring on hard ground especially if horse has upright joints.

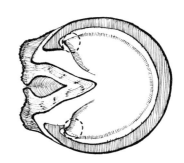

Condition	Description	Treatment	Prevention
Sprained tendon	Heat and swelling around tendon. As this swelling can also be due to an infection in the foot, if any doubt, shoe should be removed and foot checked before treating tendon.	Veterinary advice and rest is vital. Alternate hosing with cold water and poulticing with hot Animalintex, antiphlogistine or Kaolin. Blistering/firing and long rest may be necessary. Reintroduce to work gradually, with hours of walking on roads.	Avoid excessive strain and going which is deep or hard with a tired horse.
Ring-bone	Bony enlargement on pastern. Some heat and pain when worked on hard ground but often no lameness.	Rest. Cold treatment. Blistering. Consult vet.	Avoid concussion. Ensure horse is shod frequently so frog is effective as shock absorber.
Windgalls	Small swellings above fetlock joints. Very rarely causes lameness.	Massage, cold treatment, astringents, pressure bandage.	Avoid strain. Do not let toes grow very long.
Side-bone	Bony growths on cartilages in heel region. Heat and lameness.	Consult vet. Corrective shoeing. Rest and cold treatment.	Avoid excessive concussion.
Capped hock	Soft swelling on point of hock.	Hot fomentations, massage, astringent.	Remove cause, e.g. kicking when travelling (put on hock boots), scraping hock on stable floor (provide more bedding).

A strained suspensory

A bowed tendon